Civil Procedure in Russia

Civil Procedure in Russia

Third Edition

Dmitry Maleshin

This book was originally published as a monograph in the International Encyclopaedia of Laws/Civil Procedure.

Founding Editor: Roger Blanpain
General Editor: Frank Hendrickx
Volume Editor: Piet Taelman

Wolters Kluwer

Published by:
Kluwer Law International B.V.
PO Box 316
2400 AH Alphen aan den Rijn
The Netherlands
Website: www.wolterskluwerlr.com

Sold and distributed in North, Central and South America by:
Wolters Kluwer Legal & Regulatory U.S.
7201 McKinney Circle
Frederick, MD 21704
United States of America
Email: customer.service@wolterskluwer.com

Sold and distributed in all other countries by:
Quadrant
Rockwood House
Haywards Heath
West Sussex
RH16 3DH
United Kingdom
Email: international-customerservice@wolterskluwer.com

Printed on acid-free paper

ISBN 978-90-411-9212-7

e-Book: ISBN 978-90-411-9240-0
web-PDF: ISBN 978-90-411-9275-2

This title is available on www.kluwerlawonline.com

Printed and Bound by CPI Group (UK) Ltd, Croydon, CR0 4YY.

The Author

Dmitry Maleshin is a Russian scholar and author in the field of civil procedural law, legal culture, comparative law and legal education. He has authored more than 100 peer-reviewed articles as well as contributed to a number of textbooks and other works. Currently he is Professor of Civil Procedural Law at Moscow State Lomonosov University, Russia and a Visiting Professor at Saint Petersburg State University, Russia (since 2017) and National Research University Higher School of Economics, Russia (since 2014). He studied law at MSU where he received his PhD ("Candidate of Law" degree) in 2002 and DSc ("Doctor of law" degree) in 2011 by defending his thesis, "The System of the Russian Civil Justice". He has been a Visiting Scholar at Yale Law School (2004) and Harvard Law School (2008).

Prof. Maleshin is a member of numerous Russian and international associations in the field of civil procedure and legal education, International Association of Procedural Law, International Association of Judicial Independence and World Peace, etc. He engages in legislative activities in Russia and different international scholar projects. His International academic activity also includes lecturing abroad (e.g., Pavia University, Italy, 2015; Bordeaux University, France, 2016) and administrating the conferences (e.g., Moscow Congress of the IAPL, 2012; Siberian Legal Forum (Tyumen), 2014, 2016). Maleshin is a Chief Editor of the Russian Law Journal.

He also acts as a consultant and legal expert in the Russian and foreign civil procedure and ADR.

University profile: http://www.law.msu.ru/node/7344
Wikipedia: https://en.wikipedia.org/wiki/Dmitry_Maleshin
Scopus Author ID: 56601452900
ORCID: 0000-0003-2173-9800
Academia: https://moscowstate.academia.edu/DmitryMaleshin
SSRN: http://papers.ssrn.com/sol3/cf_dev/AbsByAuth.cfm?per_id=1988449SPIN: 4586-3170 h-index – 7

The Author

Table of Contents

Table of Contents

Table of Contents

List of Abbreviations

ICAC	International Commercial Arbitration Court
IP Court	Intellectual Property Court
RSFSR	Russian Soviet Federative Socialist Republic

General Introduction

§1. General Background

1. Similar civil procedural outlines exist today in Continental and Anglo-Saxon legal systems. Before addressing which attributes exist in Russia, it is necessary to note that contemporary Russian civil procedure is a mixed jurisdiction. Historically, it adhered to the civil law tradition.[1] The French Code of Civil Procedure influenced Russian prerevolution (1917) civil procedural legislation.[2] During the Soviet era judges became much more active, and this model was fairly labeled "the radical Communist solution" to the Continental civil procedure.[3] In Russia, the court could not act passively because of the widespread collective views in society.[4]

According to the Soviet Patriarch of jurisprudence Andrei Vyshinsky, the law is entirely and completely directed against exploitation and exploiters in the Soviet state; it is used as one of the means of the struggle for socialism.[5]

There are Continental features in Russian law such as case management, the absence of a jury in civil cases and the absence of class actions. Some common law features also exist in Russian civil procedure, for example, the passive role of the judge in the process of proof taking. Exceptional features of Russian civil procedure are the role of the procurator in the civil process and the review of judgments in the "supervisory" instance.

In summary then, contemporary Russian civil procedure is not a pure Continental model because it contains features of the common law procedural system as well as some other original and exceptional features.[6]

The 1990s in Russia were marked by major political and economic reforms. Those significant transformations inevitably changed relations within society, and the legal regulations that were supposed to control them demanded a considerable change as well.

A grandiose legal reform which affected all branches of law was carried out. The transformations in the sphere of civil procedure which began in the early 1990s

1. John Henry Merryman, *The Civil Law Tradition: An Introduction to the Legal Systems of Western Europe and Latin America* 121 (1969).
2. Don W. Chenworth, *Soviet Civil Procedure: History and Analysis*, 67 Trans. Amer. Phil. Soc. 3 (1977).
3. Mauro Cappelletti, *Social and Political Aspects of Civil Procedure: Reforms and Trends in Western and Eastern Europe*, 69 Mich. L. Rev. 847 (1971).
4. Harold Berman, *Justice in the USSR: An Interpretation of Soviet Law* 216–20 (1963).
5. Andrei Vyshinsky, *The Law of the Soviet State* 50 (1948).
6. Dmitry Maleshin, *The Russian Style of Civil Procedure*, 21 Emory Intl. L. Rev. 545 (2007).

are still ongoing today and have included the introduction of new legislation, from the Civil Procedural Code of the Russian Federation to enforcement laws.

§2. Delimitation of Subject Matter

I. Definition of the Term "Civil Procedure"

2. There is no definition of the term "civil procedure" in Russian legislation. At the same time, there is a discussion in Russian doctrine concerning this term.[7] Usually it defines civil procedure as the protection of violated rights in a court. The main question is: What does the word "protection" mean? Does it include enforcement proceedings or the last act of civil procedure, which is the court's decision? Most scholars argue that civil procedure does not end with the court's judgment, but requires its enforcement.[8] The final act of civil procedure according to this opinion is the bailiff's resolution on the conclusion of the enforcement proceedings.

The Russian Civil Procedural Code stipulates the tasks of civil procedure, which are: (1) protection of violated rights; (2) providing a fair hearing within a reasonable time by an independent court; (3) prevention of offenses; and (4) enhancement of respect for the rule of law and the courts.

Legislation regulating civil procedure is under the jurisdiction of the Russian Federation. "Subjects" (states) of the Federation do not have the power to regulate civil procedure.

There are separate chairs of civil procedure in most law schools. The first such chair was established in 1868 at Moscow University.

II. Distinction Between the Types of Procedure

3. There are three different types of procedure: civil, arbitrazh (commercial) and administrative. Each type of procedure is regulated by a separate code. In addition to the Civil Procedural Code (2003), there are the Arbitrazh (Commercial) Procedural Code (2002) and the Code of Administrative Procedure (2015).

The Civil Procedural Code regulates procedure relating to the disputes arising from civil, housing, family, labor and other legal relationships. Arbitrazh (commercial) procedure relates to justice in the sphere of entrepreneurial (business) and other economic activities and the settlement of economic disputes. Administrative procedure relates to the consideration of cases arising from public legal relations. For example, consideration of applications challenging legal regulations, cases relating to electoral rights protection or cases relating to the protection of the right to participate in a referendum by citizens of the Russian Federation.

7. Гражданский процесс. Под ред. М.К. Треушникова. М., 2014 (Michael Treushnikov (Ed.), Civil Procedure. 2014).
8. Гражданский процесс. Под ред. М.К. Треушникова. М., 2014 (Michael Treushnikov (Ed.), Civil Procedure. 2014).

Consideration also relates to cases in which the issue is to establish certain legal facts, the legal status of a person, the presence or absence of the indubitable rights which could be proved by a court decision. The ex parte proceeding also names the mandative proceedings as the proceedings arising from indubitable claims. For example, claims based on notarized transactions are considered mandative proceedings.

§3. Brief Historical Perspective and Sources of Civil Procedural Law

4. Current Russian civil procedural law is the result of mixing the Soviet style of adjudication with the prerevolutionary laws of the nineteenth century, as well as with modern international standards. Some features are unique, with their roots in ancient Russian laws and traditions. Moreover, the specificity of the legal culture should also be taken into account.

Historically, Russian civil procedure has been close to the European continental system. Different parts of the Russian system were adopted in different historical periods: Byzantine law (ninth–tenth century); Swedish law (eighteenth century); French law (eighteenth–nineteenth century); and German law (nineteenth–twentieth century).

The first written legal act was the trade agreement entered into between Prince Oleg and the Byzantine Empire in AD 911. Byzantium had a significant economic, trade and cultural influence on the Kievan Rus during that time. Slavs adopted many Byzantine legal institutions, especially criminal procedure and evidence.

5. Codified acts play the key role in the subsequent history of Russian civil procedure. Some of them are completely devoted to civil legal proceedings; some contain only a special section on this matter. Those documents are:

- Russkaia Pravda, eleventh century.
- The Pskov Judicial Charter (Pskovskaia Sudnaia Gramota), 1397.
- The Novgorod Judicial Charter (Novgorodskaia Sudnaia Gramota), 1471.
- The Law Code (Sudebnik), 1497.
- The Law Code (Sudebnik), 1550.
- The Sobornoe Ulozhenie, 1649.
- The Civil Procedure Code of the Russian Empire (Ustav Grazhdanskogo sudoproisvodstva), 1864.
- The Civil Procedure Code of the RSFSR (Russian Soviet Federative Socialist Republic), 1923.
- The Civil Procedure Code of the RSFSR (Russian Soviet Federative Socialist Republic), 1964.
- The Civil Procedural Code of the Russian Federation, 2003.

Russkaia Pravda contains a number of rules on civil evidence and litigation. The power to consider cases belonged only to the Prince. Some rules on evidence were original, and some were adopted from Byzantine law.

With the adoption of Christianity, canon law (also from Byzantium) began to play a very important role. It regulated marriage, divorce, and all family conflicts.

Two key acts entered into force in the fourteenth–fifteenth century: the Pskov Judicial Charter (Pskovskaia Sudnaia Gramota) of 1397 and the Novgorod Judicial Charter (Novgorodskaia Sudnaia Gramota) of 1471. They were enacted despite the dominion of the Tatar-Mongol Yoke; most legal procedures originated from the Russkaia Pravda, and Mongol litigation practices were not adopted.

The Judicial Code (Sudebnik) of 1497 and the Judicial Code (Sudebnik) of 1550 started to regulate the judicial procedure in a more detailed manner than previously. The main judicial power belonged, as before, to the Prince. There were also regional governors who had the right to consider some cases, but their decisions could be appealed to the Prince. There were also different judicial officials who assisted in consideration of cases. The main evidence used in civil cases was witness testimony. Judicial duels were also widespread. Proceedings during that time were adversarial.

The Sobornoe Ulozhenie of 1649 is the most important legal act of medieval Russia. It is an example of the first structural codification of civil procedural law in Russia. It was influenced not only by previous norms based on Byzantine law but also by the legislation of the Lithuanian Code of 1588. That same Code, moreover, directly applied in a number of north- and south-western Muscovite territories.[9] The proceedings remained adversarial in nature.

6. The next important step was the modernization of the Russian legal system by Peter the Great. Modernization during that period is usually described as Westernization. Sweden served as an example for many changes, including legal changes. Civil procedure was also updated in accordance with Swedish legislation. This ended the adversarial model and introduced an inquisitorial model.

The Great Judicial Reform of 1864 was a major legal event in the prerevolutionary period. It was initiated by Tsar Alexander II and is treated as a part of his Great Reforms in accordance with his political and economic reforms agenda. It abolished previous legislation and established a new model. Civil procedure became oral and adversarial. Justices of the peace and professional attorneys were introduced. Courts and judges acquired genuine independence. Practices of litigation changed radically.

The Reform concerned the judicial system; but civil and criminal procedures, as well as civil and criminal laws, were also reformed within a few years of its launch. It was a very important reform for Russian society. Most legal institutions were not only updated but also reestablished. A new legal landscape was created for the huge country.

7. The Reform touched the territory not only of contemporary Russia but also of the modern countries of Poland, Finland, Ukraine and Belorussia, and the states of the Caucasus and the Baltic regions. Its legal background has not only Russian national juridical roots but also French, German, Austrian and Italian influence. Therefore, the Reform has not only national (Russian) dimensions but also a common trans-European sense. It should be seen as a common European and Eurasian legal event, one that influenced the legislation and legal culture of many countries in the region during a substantial time period. For example, the Russian Civil Procedure Code was in effect

9. M. Kovalevsky, *Modern Customs and Ancient Laws of Russia* 51 (1891).

until 1933 in Poland[10] and until 1940 in Lithuania[11] (sixteen and twenty-three years after the collapse of the Russian Empire). Most of its parts were copied, with only the names changed, by the Soviet authorities during the drafting of the USSR codes.

The Great Judicial Reform is treated as one of the most successful innovations of Tsar Alexander II. It was undertaken owing to the influence of the West on Russia.[12] It began in November 1864, but it was preceded by more than ten years of intricate drafting work. The drafting committee was established at the beginning of the 1850s and included a number of well-known Russian lawyers. The first result of this work was the prepared conception of innovations that was adopted by the Tsar on September 29, 1862. The document was titled "General provisions of judicial reforms," and after publication it received huge public discussion: 446 proposals were submitted to the drafting committee from judges, prosecutors and attorneys. Final drafts were signed by the Tsar on November 20, 1864. Four statutes were adopted: Statute of Judicial Institutions; Criminal Procedure Code; Civil Procedure Code; and Statute on Punishments. A few years following implementation of the reform, all of the drafting papers were collected into seventy-four volumes.

The drafts were greatly influenced by the ideas of the Russian jurist Michael Speransky (1772–1839) who tried to reform Russian law in 1820s, as well as by the new European codes of the second half of the nineteenth century. The main idea of the Reform was expressed by Alexander II in his statement that he wished "to introduce into Russia legal proceedings that are swift, just, merciful and equal for all" (Decree of November 20, 1864).

8. The new Russian judicial system of that time was based on the following principles: an independent judiciary, oral and adversarial trial, equality of all before the law, introduction of legal representation, an educated legal profession, an independent bar association, jury trial for serious criminal cases and justices of the peace.

Judicial Reform marked a shift in Russian from an amorphous, corrupt system of procedure to an independent, modern system as liberal as any nation in Europe.[13] However, two aspects of the Reform can be viewed in a negative light. First, the Reform was realized in the main towns of the country and did not extend the court system into the villages, where traditional peasant justice continued to operate with minimal influence from the government. The new court system was effective, but it was realized only with respect to 20% of the population because 80% were peasants.

Second, the codes did not have effective practice. They were among the best European codes but were unsuccessful in Russia. One may reasonably agree with many Russian and foreign scholars who argue that norms which are successful for

---

10. Piotr Rylski & Karol Weitz, *The Impact of the Russian Civil Judicial Proceedings Act of 1864 on Polish Civil Proceedings*, 2(4) Russian L.J. 82 (2014).
11. Dalia Mikulėnienė & Valentinas Mikelėnas, *Reception of Russian Statute of Civil Procedure of 1864 in Lithuania during 1918–1940*, 2(4) Russian L.J. 105 (2014).
12. Vladimir Przhilenskiy & Maria Zakharova, *Which Way is the Russian Double-Headed Eagle Looking?*, 4(2) Russian L.J. 12 (2016).
13. Brian Conlon, *Dostoevsky v. the Judicial Reforms of 1864 : How and Why One of Nineteenth-Century Russia's Greatest Writers Criticized the Nation's Most Successful Reform*, 2(4) Russian L.J. 8 (2014).

Europe do not necessarily work properly in Russia.[14] The Civil Procedure Code is a good example. Twenty years after its adoption, a special drafting committee was established to prepare a new code.

In spite of these negatives, the Reform made the Russian judicial system open, adversarial and more professional. It could be treated as the starting point of a new period in the history of the Russian judiciary that continues to the present day. Contemporary Russian civil and criminal procedure, notary, justices of the peace, juries, etc. all of the major aspects of these institutions have their roots in 1864.

9. Soviet civil procedure (1917–1991) was radically inquisitorial. Soviet judges were more active than their European civil law counterparts. Proceedings were overseen in accordance with the principle of "objective" (material) truth. Objective truth is usually used in civil procedure doctrine in contrast to formal truth. Material truth was an important part of Soviet legality. This principle was crucial in evidence gathering. The main task was to find objective truth. A judge was obliged to ascertain the truth and, therefore, had the power to obtain any evidence that he needed to consider the case.

In addition to the judge's activity, there were some other particular features of the Soviet civil procedure. First, procurators had immense powers. The Procurator General could initiate the inspection of any case considered by a court. Second, there was an additional appeals stage called "supervisory proceedings." Supervisory proceedings were similar to cassation but could be initiated by certain official authorities as well as the parties.

10. The new Constitution of the Russian Federation was approved in 1993. It was adopted by national referendum on December 12, 1993 with 54.5% of the vote, and it took effect on the day it was published—25 December of the same year. The new Constitution set out the fundamentals of government as well as proclaiming the rule of law, the ideological neutrality of the state, political pluralism, competitive elections and separation of powers, and guaranteeing fundamental human rights to the Russian people. It also proclaimed a number of important principles of civil procedure such as the independence of judges, adversarial proceedings and orality.

11. The new Civil Procedural Code was adopted in 2003 after ten years of official drafting. There is also the Arbitrazh (Commercial) Procedural Code (2002) and the Code of Administrative Procedure (2015).

Precedent is not the source of the law; however, the acts of the Supreme Court and Constitutional Court are applied not only by lower-instance courts but also by governmental authorities.

International accords are also a source of civil procedural law. Russia is a party to nearly forty multilateral and bilateral international treaties, conventions and agreements on legal aid rendering in civil and commercial cases, binding the Russian Federation and more than 100 signatory states with international obligations. According to the Constitution (Article 15), if the provisions of Russian legislation conflict with international treaty, the provisions of international treaty will be applied.

Some of the most considerable multilateral international treaties containing legal procedural norms are the following:

14. Harold J. Berman, *Justice in the U.S.S.R.: An Interpretation of Soviet Law* 216 (1963).

- Hague Convention of March 1, 1954, on Civil Procedure.
- Hague Convention of November 15, 1965, on Service Abroad of Judicial and Extra-Judicial Documents in Civil and Commercial Matters.
- Hague Convention of March 18, 1970, on the Taking of Evidence Abroad in Civil or Commercial Matters.

The Soviet Union joined the Convention of 1954 in 1967, and the Russian Federation joined the Conventions of 1965 and 1970 in 2001. Forty-one states currently participate in the Hague Conventions. A considerable number of bilateral international treaties were signed by the Soviet Union, and Russia is a party to those as the successor state.

§4. General Principles of Civil Procedural Law

12. In Russia, the principles of civil procedure are the fundamental guarantees of civil justice; they are its guiding ideas. Principles establish the content and structure of civil procedural law. They define the aims of procedure and the methods by which to achieve those aims, they characterize the content of the activities of legal entities in civil procedural law and they define the essential features expressing the essence of procedural law. The principles of civil procedural law represent not simply a group of principles, rather they form a certain set or system. The reason for that lies in the unity of the ideas expressed in the principles, in their tendency to attain the unified aim, and this emphasizes the public nature of civil procedure.

As an example of this close correlation it is possible to point out the principle of an oral nature of civil procedure. The oral nature ensures a direct perception of the majority of evidence, and that promotes the emergence of the principle of direct examination of evidence. In addition, the oral nature gives to everyone present in the courtroom the chance to follow the judicial examination process and to perceive all the factual background of the case, i.e. it provides the principle of the public nature of judicial proceedings, of openness and to a certain point the principle of adversarial proceedings, and the principle of the rule of law.

13. Each of the principles plays an independent role in the stages of proceedings or their separate institutes.

The independence of justice is one of the main principles of civil procedure. It is established in the Constitution as well as in the procedural codes. This means that when administering justice, judges are independent and there may be no external influence on judges and interference with their activities by public authorities, local governmental bodies, and state officials is forbidden.

Another principle is a reasonable time for consideration of a case and for the enforcement of a judgment. When reasonable time is estimated, such circumstances as the legal and factual complexity of the case, the behavior of the parties to the proceedings, the sufficiency and efficiency of the court's actions should be taken into account. Parties are entitled to file an application with the chairman of the court to speed up the consideration of the case. This application should be decided upon within five days of its receipt and result in the chairman of the court fixing the time for the consideration of the case or indicating the actions that should be performed to speed up the consideration of the case.

The principle of equality of arms of the parties means that the parties enjoy equal rights regarding recusals and motions, introduction of evidence, participation in the examination of evidence and in pleadings, presentation of their arguments and explanations to the court, as well as the exercise of their procedural rights. Parties to the proceedings are equal before the law and the court regardless of sex, race, nationality, language, property status or attitude in respect of religion. There is also equality of all organizations before the law regardless of their legal form, form of property or location. The court is not entitled to give any privileges to any of the parties or, by its actions, to derogate the rights of one of the parties.

One of the major principles is the principle of the adversarial nature of the proceedings. It is enshrined in Article 123 of the Constitution. This principle defines the competitive nature of all civil legal proceedings. The adversarial process symbolizes the equality of the parties which is emphasized in paragraph 3 Article 123 of the Constitution and in Article 12 of the Civil Procedural Code. Parties can compete in court only if they are equal in defending their rights and legitimate interests in the introduction of evidence.

14. The parties at trial present the facts connected with the emergence, enforcement or termination of a right, and data relating to these facts. This moment is a key difference between competitive procedure and investigative (inquisitional) procedure, where the parties and persons concerned have no right to produce evidence, and the judicial authorities have the duty of evidence collection.

In Russia, the investigative procedure was established by Decree of February 21, 1697 of Peter the Great. The Decree emphasized that there would be investigation instead of courtroom confrontation. But after twenty-six years in his new Decree of November 5, 1723 investigation was abolished owing to numerous judicial abuses. However, some elements of the investigative process still remained. According to the current Civil Procedural Code (paragraph 2 Article 12), the court explains to the participants in the case their rights and duties, and warns them of the effects of their performance of procedural actions or failure to do so. In this regard, we consider that there is no need to name the equality of the parties as an independent principle. After all, the equality of the parties is introduced into the process for the purpose of an adversarial nature of the proceedings, and therefore the principles of adversarial proceedings and the equality of arms of the parties have to be unified.

The Civil Procedural Code does not mention truth as a principle of civil procedural law. Civil courts in Russia are not required by law to find the truth.[15] The absence of the direct instruction to discover the truth in civil cases does not mean that the court does not do so. The court's decision has to be based on the established truth, on the facts proved during the court sessions. The fact that the truth is established in the competitive process as well as in the investigative process can be derived from many norms of the Civil Procedural Code. In a civil case, the court renders assistance in the exercise of the parties' rights; it creates the conditions for a comprehensive and full examination of the evidence, for the establishment of the facts and for the correct

15. Ruth van der Pol & Anton Petrov, *Searching for truth in civil process: The Netherlands and Russia*, 3(1) Russian L.J. 121 (2015).

application of law during consideration and adjudication of civil cases. The court must help the parties with defining the subject of proof, i.e. to name the circumstances connected to the existence or absence of rights and to name the party who has to prove them. Furthermore, the court cannot refuse satisfaction of a declared motion for the request of relevant proofs.

15. The principle of discretion (or the principle of the free exercise of material and procedural rights by the parties to legal proceedings since "optionality" is not a Western legal concept), like the principle of adversarial proceedings, is one of the most important principles of civil procedure. The essence of the principle of discretion in civil procedural law is in the freedom of the parties to dispose of their material and procedural rights, and, as already mentioned, the court assists them in the exercise of those rights. Actions by the parties are designed for the emergence of the procedure (filing a complaint), for process development (filing an appeal) or for process termination (e.g., a settlement agreement between the parties). This nature of discretion allows us to say that it is the driving force in civil procedure.

To repeat then, discretion concerns issues of emergence, development and termination of the procedure.

The essence of the principle of discretion is revealed in many norms of the Civil Procedural Code. It is revealed through the definition of the subject, the grounds of an action, the application of the grounds, the increase or reduction of the size of the claim and the renunciation of the suit. At such affirmative performance the court checks the legality of such actions, and it investigates as to whether they are intended towards infringement of someone's rights and legitimate interests. The court cannot satisfy the claims which were not stated by the party. Through these actions the discretion in material law is shown.

16. In procedural law, discretion is revealed where there is no order of material law; for example, the application for a provisional remedy, a statement for providing the claim, filing the cassational appeal, a motion for an examination. Normally, persons concerned take the initiative in the commission of discretional actions. The court is obliged to warn of the effects of performance of procedural actions or failure to do so.

The publicity of civil proceedings is regulated in a very detailed manner in Russian law. First, courts and proceedings are open to the public. Second, cases may be considered *in camera* if their consideration in open sessions may lead to the divulgence of a state secret, as well as in the event of satisfaction of a motion of a party which refers to the necessity of keeping commercial, official or other secrets. It is also possible to make notes and audio recordings during open sessions. Filming, photography and videotape recording are allowed only with permission of the judge. Third, judgments are publicly pronounced and are available through official online judicial systems. Confidential proceedings take place when state secrets or the secret of the adoption of a child are the objects of investigation or one of the parties requests confidential proceedings such as commercial secret in order to preserve information that is protected by the law.

The official language of proceedings is Russian, as it is the official language of the Russian Federation. Civil proceedings in the "subjects" (states) of the Federation may be conducted in the official language of the "subject," which could be other than Russian. Proceedings in military courts are conducted only in the Russian language.

Parties who do not know the official language of the proceedings have the right to use the services of an interpreter.

Part I. Judicial Organization: The Courts and Their Members

Chapter 1. The Courts and Their Members

§1. The Courts

I. Structure of the Court System

17. The Russian judiciary is regulated by special Chapter 7 "Judiciary" of the Constitution as well as by the special laws "On the Judicial System" (1996), "On Courts of General Jurisdiction" (2011), "On Commercial Courts" (1995) and "On the Status of Judges in the Russian Federation" (1992).

Today the Russian civil judiciary is composed of the courts of general jurisdiction, military courts, commercial courts and the Intellectual Property Court (IP Court). The main law governing the fundamental principles of the Russian court system is the Law "On the Judicial System of the Russian Federation" (1996).

Arbitrazh (commercial) courts are charged with settling economic disputes, while courts of general jurisdiction handle disputes between individual citizens. The arbitrazh court system was established in 1991 after the collapse of the Soviet Union and the adoption of a market economy. Arbitrazh courts are structured as a three-tier system. The main law governing the activity of arbitrazh courts is the Law "On Arbitrazh Courts in the Russian Federation" (1995). Arbitrazh courts also have exclusive jurisdiction over the recognition and enforcement of foreign court decisions and arbitral awards. There are four levels in the system of arbitrazh courts: eighty-five regional courts, twenty-one appellate courts, ten territorial (cassation) courts and the Supreme Court. Regional arbitrazh (commercial) courts also have internal division in relation to the specialization of judges. There are, for example, bankruptcy, administrative special panels of judges.

18. The competence of the courts of general jurisdiction includes civil disputes, appeals of administrative actions, labor and employment disputes, family law and consumer protection, among other types of cases. There is a general rule that all cases not referred to the arbitrazh courts are handled by the courts of general jurisdiction. The main law governing the activity of the courts of general jurisdiction is the Law

"On the Courts of General Jurisdiction of the Russian Federation". There are three levels in the system of the courts of general jurisdiction: district courts, regional courts and the Supreme Court. District courts are established based on the administrative divisions of a region and regional courts operate on the level of the region (i.e., a subject of the Federation). There are eighty-five regions in Russia.

Justices of the peace handle property disputes with an amount of claim under RUR 50,000 and some types of family cases.

Military courts deal with civil cases that fall under the jurisdiction of the courts of general jurisdiction that occur while service in the military services is involved.

Owing to its adherence to international treaties, Russia is subject to the jurisdiction of the European Court of Human Rights and the Court of the Eurasian Economic Community.

II. Supreme Court of the Russian Federation

19. The Supreme Court is the highest court for all courts in Russia. It was established in 1923 as the Supreme Court of the USSR and in 1992 it began to function as the highest court of the Russian Federation.

Depending on the case, the Supreme Court may handle appeal, cassation and supervisory cases, as well as act as a Court of First Instance. One of the tasks of the Supreme Court is the harmonization of judicial practice. In carrying out this task it reviews and analyzes court practice, and as a result of this activity it may issue clarifications and interpretations of the law.

The most important and widely reported legal event in Russia of the last five years was the reform of the Supreme Court, which in fact saw the unification of the Supreme Court and the Supreme Arbitrazh (Commercial) Court.

20. Until 2013 there had been two parallel Supreme Courts in Russia: the Supreme Court and the Supreme Arbitrazh (Commercial) Court. This changed in 2014 when the two courts were united. This reform was undertaken at the initiative of President Vladimir Putin under the bill titled "About the Supreme Court of the Russian Federation and Prosecutor's Office of the Russian Federation," which regulates the structure of the Russian judicial system, and which changed the Constitution for the second time since its adoption. The Supreme Arbitrazh (Commercial) Court was abolished and its functions transferred to the Supreme Court. This reform idea proved highly controversial. With advantages and disadvantages, it was hotly debated among lawyers and members of the judicial community, attracting criticism from some. More than 100 law offices signed a petition to stop the reform's progress, arguing that the work of the Supreme Arbitrazh (Commercial) Court had been most effective. On the other hand, authors of the reform asserted the need to eliminate differences and contradictions in the judicial practice of both Supreme Courts.

A number of laws were adopted with amendments to the Russian legislation in relation to the unification of both high courts. Except organizational changes there was a big block of procedural, financial and administrative changes. Supreme Arbitrazh court was excluded from the list of courts and regional federal arbitrazh courts were renamed as just regional arbitrazh courts.

21. The new united Supreme Court of the Russian Federation began its work in August 2014. It has a new structure and consists of 170 judges, including the Chief Justice, and chairmen of six chambers, which are: an Appeals chamber, a Judicial chamber for criminal cases, a Judicial chamber for civil cases, a Judicial chamber for economic cases, a Judicial chamber for administrative cases and a Military chamber. The Supreme Arbitrazh Court had its functions suspended in August 2014, but the entire arbitrazh court system is still working. The Judicial chamber on economic cases acts as the final instance for economic cases considered in arbitrazh (commercial) courts.

The Plenum of the Supreme Court consists of all judges of the Supreme Court. The Plenum deals with the most complicated matters regarding the functioning of the general jurisdiction courts and the administration of justice. The Plenum reviews and clarifies information on the application of legal practice and decides matters on the introduction of legal initiatives as well as on requests to the Constitutional Court of the Russian Federation regarding constitutional law and the verification of other legal acts. The Plenum also approves the composition of the judicial chambers, the panels and the secretary of the Plenum, and the Scientific and Consulting Council under the Supreme Court of the Russian Federation. The Prosecutor General and the Minister of Justice can participate in the Plenum sessions. They or their substitutes have the right to make correspondent introductions to be heard during the Plenum sessions. They also have the right to express their opinions on the matters in discussion. Plenum sessions should be organized to take place at least once in every four months.

22. The Presidium of the Supreme Court is the highest and the final judicial instance for cases viewed under general jurisdiction. The Presidium consists of the Chief Justice and his deputies. Among the members of the Presidium of the Supreme Court are some of the most respected judges of the Supreme Court. The total number of Presidium members is thirteen. The composition of the Presidium is approved upon introduction by the President of the Russian Federation, based on the presentation of the Chief Justice and a positive resolution by the Highest Qualification Panel of Judges. The Presidium of the Supreme Court hears cases when the majority of its members are present. The Supreme Court has original jurisdiction in certain cases. Those cases include: challenges to individual acts of the Federal Assembly and decrees by the President of Russia and the government of Russia; challenges to delegated legislation of governmental agencies; termination of political parties and all-Russian NGOs; challenges to actions of the Central Electoral Commission of Russia when organizing presidential elections, State Duma (Russia's parliament) elections or referendums. The Supreme Court may also hear criminal cases against members of the Federation Council of Russia and the State Duma, and federal judges, at its discretion. Presidium sessions should be organized to take place at least once each month.

23. The Academic Consultative Council is a body created to assist the Supreme Court in various legal and academic matters. It comprises members of the Supreme Court itself, academics, practicing lawyers and law enforcement officers. Its composition is approved by the Plenum; it is presided over by the Chief Justice. The Scientific and Consulting Council elaborates scientifically based recommendations on the most complex and important issues of judicial practice. These recommendations may be elaborated as preparation for the clarifications by the Plenum on issues of judicial practice, law projects and preparation of other legal acts, and in respect of specific case trials.

There are also a large number of clerks working in agencies and departments who deal with matters such as the analysis of judicial practice, legislation, personnel and state services, administration, planning and finance, economics, legal information and international law.

III. Intellectual Property Court

24. The IP Court is a specialized Russian court. It acts as a part of the commercial courts system. The scope of its competence covers disputes connected to intellectual rights.

This category of disputes is notable not only for the complexity of the legal analysis but also for the complexity of technical issues connected with the specifics of intellectual rights. Handling a case not only requires serious experience in legal practice but also requires skills in technical spheres. The judge considering such a case usually needs to understand some technical issues connected with intellectual property rights. The specialized IP Court provides efficiency of judicial proceedings by means of specialization of judicial practice in this area. Narrow specialization of judges increases the quality of judicial work and reduces the consideration time of a case.

25. The Russian IP Court was established in 2011. However, the idea of a specialized IP court was announced for the first time in the late 1980s. Prior to its creation, there were a number of drafts on this topic and even some laws supported this idea and contained the provisions concerning the necessity to establish a specialized IP court. The creation of the Patent Court of the USSR was stipulated in the 1988 Law "On Inventive Activity in the USSR" (Articles 55, 56), in the 1991 USSR Law "On Inventions in the USSR" (Articles 14, 15, 25, 42, 43), in the 1991 USSR Law "On Industrial Models" (Article 26), in the 1991 USSR Law "On Trademarks and Service Marks" (Article 32). The USSR Law "On the Patent Court of the USSR" did not come into force. The Concept of Judicial Reform in the Russian Federation (1991) designated a need for court specialization and judicial specialization. The 1992 Law "On Trademarks" provided for the creation of the Patent Court of the Russian Federation. However, the legislator refused this idea in favor of an administrative order on dispute settlement in this area. In 2010, the project of the Federal Constitutional Law "On Patent Courts of the Russian Federation" providing for the formation of an independent patent court system was brought to the State Duma, but was not accepted. The initiative for creating today's IP Court was that of the Supreme Commercial Court of the Russian Federation, which even adopted a special Plenum Resolution in 2013 on this court's functioning.

The IP Court sits in Moscow. The structure of the Court consists of the presiding judge, two deputies, a presidium and two judicial panels. There is also an Academic and Advisory Council. The Court uses the Arbitrazh (Commercial) Procedural Code as the procedural rules for considering cases.

The IP Court acts as both a Court of First Instance and a court of cassation. Despite the fact that the IP Court is part of the commercial court system, the criteria of jurisdiction of commercial courts do not apply to it: its competence does not depend on the nature of the dispute (economic or personal) or on the status of the subject to a dispute (citizen, legal entity or sole trader).

As a Court of First Instance, the IP Court considers: cases of contest of legislative acts of the federal government in the sphere of intellectual property; and cases of disputes on intellectual property activity. As a court of cassation, it considers: cases previously considered in the IP Court as a Court of First Instance; and cases in the sphere of intellectual property decided by arbitrazh (commercial) courts.

IV. Juries

26. Jury trial is one of the controversial questions of the Russian legal system. Jury trial was first introduced in Russia in the second half of the nineteenth century. It was a part of the Great Judicial Reform of 1864, together with the introduction of professional judges and attorneys, notaries public, and civil and criminal procedural reforms.

Anglo-Saxon legislation served as the model for the Russian jury at that time. These early jury trials were only implemented in Saint Petersburg and Moscow. Only men could be appointed as jury members. The court with jury had the power to consider 410 offenses according to the Russian Criminal Code. That is around 20% of all offenses. In 1878, several offenses were excluded from the competence of the jury, e.g. murders of officials and breaches of the peace. A jury consisted of twelve persons; it was independent from the professional judge and did not participate in civil cases.

In 1917, jury trials were abolished by the Soviet government and lay assessors replaced juries. This model was borrowed from the German Schöffen model. Two lay assessors considered criminal and civil cases together with a single professional judge. They served for a term of two and a half years. In contrast to the jury member, the Soviet lay assessor had the power to consider, together with a judge, not only the determination of a fact but also the meaning of a law.

In 1993, jury trial was reintroduced in Russia by the Constitution (Articles 20, 32, 47, 123). The current Russian jury system is a mix of the nineteenth century-model and Anglo-Saxon legislation. A jury's jurisdiction is limited to aggravated murder, racketeering, aggravated bribery and crimes against justice. Juries are not involved in civil cases and cannot consider crimes against the state.

At trial, a jury consists of twelve members. They are selected from a list of fifty candidates who must be at least twenty-five years of age and must not have criminal records. The judge pronounces the decision in the case on the basis of the jury's verdict. In December 2015, President Putin proposed reducing the number of jurors to between five and seven.

Here are some interesting jury-related statistics. Pilot juries were implemented in 1993–1994 in nine federal regions. Currently, jury trials operate in all regions. The last region to introduce trial by jury was Chechnya in 2010. In 1993, juries considered two cases, in 1994 they considered 173 cases. Currently they consider around 500 cases annually, which is approximately 1% of all criminal cases.

V. Judicial Statistics

27. In Russia in 2013 there were around 2,500 courts of general jurisdiction and 111 arbitrazh (commercial) courts; and around 30,000 judges, including 4,000 arbitrazh (commercial) judges and 7,400 justices of the peace.

Cases in arbitrazh court, whether in a Court of First Instance, appellate instance or cassational instance, last around nine months. In practice, the court may accelerate the proceedings and the claimant may not pass through all judicial stages, so cases often last around five or six months. Cases in a court of general jurisdiction last two or three months for a simple case, such as one for recovery of costs for damage caused by a car accident, and can last some years for complicated cases, such as one over inheritance or a real estate dispute, but generally last around six to eight months.

VI. Administration of the Court

28. According to the Constitution (Article 118), justice in Russia is administered by the courts alone. The independence of judges is considered a separate constitutional principle (Article 122) as it concerns the personal security of the judge, members of his family, his dwelling and property, and also his office. The judge is granted the right for the storage and carrying of firearms. The financing of the courts comes from the federal budget and must provide for the possibility of the full and independent implementation of justice. Additionally, there is a special law "About additional guarantees of social protection of judges and workers of courts' offices of the Russian Federation" (1996).

VII. Public Prosecutor's Office

29. The public prosecutor is an active participant in civil procedures, as well as in commercial (arbitrazh) and administrative procedures. His participation in court proceedings is a separate competence according to the Law "On the Public Prosecution Service of the Russian Federation" (1992).

There are three forms of participation of the public prosecutor in civil procedures. First, the public prosecutor has the right to appeal to the court in order to protect the public interests and the rights of Russian Federation (Article 45 Civil Procedural Code). Second, the public prosecutor can sue a case to protect the rights of citizens who cannot apply to the court themselves due to health reasons, age, incapacity and other substantiated reasons. Third, the public prosecutor should give his legal opinion on a limited number of cases to protect social and labor rights, family, motherhood, paternity and childhood, health rights, including medical care, environmental and educational rights.

The public prosecutor who submits a claim acts as the claimant, meaning *inter alia* that he has to prove with those circumstances to which he refers.

The role pf public prosecutor in commercial (arbitrazh) procedures is different. His main task here is to protect public interests in economic relations. According to the Commercial (Arbitrazh) Procedural Code he is entitled to file a claim: (1) to dispute laws and legal acts of federal and local authorities in relation to entrepreneurial and other economic activities; (2) for applying the effects of invalidity of a void transaction made by governmental or municipal organizations.

§2. Members of the Judiciary

I. Appointment of Judges

30. All judges of the federal courts are appointed to their position according to Article 128 of the Constitution. Depending on the level of the courts, some judges are appointed by the Federation Council of the Federal Assembly of the Russian Federation and others by the President of the Russian Federation. In order to become a judge, a person must be a citizen of Russia, be at least twenty-five years old, have a university degree in law and have at least five years of legal service. Before presenting the applicant for the judge's position, there is a preliminary coordination of the candidacy with the qualifications commission of judges. The Highest Qualifications Panel of Judges is a nongovernmental organization of the Russian judiciary that plays a key role in the appointment, promotion and dismissal of judges.

The Chairman of the Supreme Court of the Russian Federation is nominated by the President of Russia and appointed by the Federal Council of the Federal Assembly of the Russian Federation for a six-year term. The deputy chairmen of the Supreme Court and other judges of the Court are appointed similarly, but the President's nomination is based on the nomination by the Chairman of the Supreme Court.

All other federal judges—from chairmen of the regional courts to judges of district courts—are appointed to their positions by the President upon nomination by the Chairman of the Supreme Court in coordination with the qualifications commission of judges and with the opinion of the regional parliaments.

Chapter 2. The Bar

§1. Legal Education

31. Students are usually 16–17 years old when they start to study law in Russia. After four years of education in a bachelors program, students may conclude their studies or continue to study at the same university or at another one in or outside of Russia. There is a list of 200 foreign universities whose degrees are valid in Russia without any additional approval. Bachelor and Master's degrees require passing a state examination as well as submission of a qualified dissertation. Bar admission is required for attorneys, notaries and judges. Finally, there are two postgraduate law degrees: candidate of law and doctor of law.

The first law faculty was established in 1755 at Moscow University, now named Lomonosov Moscow State University. The first law professors were invited from Europe. In the nineteenth century there were seven main universities with law faculties in the Russian Empire: in Moscow, Saint Petersburg, Kazan, Kiev, Warsaw, Vilnius and Tartu. During Soviet times there were around fifty law schools in the USSR.

Nowadays there are approximately 1,200 law schools. These include both state and private universities. During the last several years the following gradation scale has occurred: Russia has different types of higher education institutions including national university, federal university, national research university, university, academy and institute. Institutions may be state-run or private. Law faculties exist in most institutions.

The law courses are usually based on the national legal system as well as international law, theory and history of law. Foreign law is rarely studied, but it is the subject of many research papers. Ninety-five percent of the programs are in Russian and only very few law schools provide legal courses in English. Most professors are Russian, as the use of foreign visiting scholars is not popular. As a rule, there are no academic legal courses joined with foreign universities.

Legal clinics comprise one of the components of the practical training of the Russian lawyer. These clinics appeared in the mid-1990s and were considered progressive educational technology. Historically, Russia's first legal clinic was established at Kazan University in the 1840s, at the initiative of Professor Dmitry Meyer.

32. It is important to note that the Russian educational model has European roots. The history of modern Russian legal education starts in the eighteenth century with the first Russian university founded in 1755 in Moscow (Lomonosov Moscow State University) with three faculties: law, philosophy and medicine. The first professor of law was Philipp Heinrich Dilthey, who was invited from Vienna University and served as the only professor of law for ten years. The first Russian professors of law, Semen Desnitskii and Ivan Tretiakov, studied abroad in Glasgow, Scotland and began teaching courses in 1767. Since Desnitskii and Tretiakov could lecture in Russian, the number of law students increased appreciably. Russian universities of the eighteenth and nineteenth centuries were established following the Western example. Some of the first professors of law, invited from abroad, taught in foreign languages. In addition, of course, there were local professors, but almost all of them were trained and defended their theses abroad (e.g., in Germany, England). Russian legal writings in the nineteenth century were very similar to European legal writing, especially to those in the French and German academy.

§2. Exercise of the Legal Profession

33. The attorney is determined by the law as an independent legal counsel.

I. Conditions for Admission

34. An attorney's license is available to a person with a law degree or a postgraduate law degree. It is also necessary to have at least two years of practice in law. A person meeting these requirements is entitled to apply to the qualifications commission of a bar association of the Russian Federation state for a law license. The qualifications commission arranges the verification of the applicant's paperwork and disclosures. No applicant can be denied to sit the bar exam. The bar exam consists of a written test and an interview. An applicant who fails the bar exam must wait one year before retaking the exam. The qualifications commission may not deny a law license to an applicant who passes the bar exam. A license is granted for life.

An applicant who passes the bar exam takes the following oath: "I solemnly swear that I will honestly and in good faith perform the duties of lawyer, protect the rights, freedoms and interests of clients pursuant to the Constitution of the Russian Federation, the law and the code of ethics of the legal profession." As of the day of the oath, the applicant is licensed to practice law and admitted to the bar. The only documentary evidence of admission to practice law is the certificate, issued by the qualifications commission.

35. An attorney's license will be suspended for the following reasons: (1) the attorney is elected to public office (for the term of office); or (2) the attorney is unable to perform his professional duties for more than six months. An attorney will be disbarred by the bar council in the Russian Federation for the following reasons: (1) the attorney files a disbarment request with the bar council; (2) the attorney is declared incapable or impaired by a court decision; (3) the attorney dies or a court decision declaring him dead becomes final; or (4) a judgment finding the attorney guilty of a premeditated crime becomes final. The attorney can be disbarred by resolution of the bar council in the Russian Federation state on whose state register the lawyer's details are entered based on the qualifications commission's finding where: (a) the attorney is in breach of his professional duties to a client; (b) the attorney is in breach of the code of ethics of the legal profession; (c) the attorney fails to comply with the decisions of the bar association authorities made within their purview; (d) misrepresentations are discovered in the disclosures made to the qualifications commission; or (e) no details of the form of legal practice chosen by the lawyer are received by the bar association.

II. Rights and Duties

36. According to the Federal Law "On the practice of law and the legal profession in the Russian Federation" an attorney has the right to: (1) collect the information necessary for the provision of legal assistance, and specifically to request statements, references and other documents from federal and local authorities; (2) interview, subject to their consent, any persons believed to have information germane to the case in which the attorney is providing legal assistance; (3) collect and provide objects and documents that may be deemed to be physical and other evidence; (4) contract experts to elucidate matters related to the provision of legal assistance; (5) meet with a client in private unopposed in confidential surroundings (including when held in custody), with no limit on the number or duration of visits; and (6) document (including technologically) the contents of the file on the case in which the attorney is providing legal assistance, with due regard for state and other legally protected secrets.

An attorney may not: (1) undertake to do anything patently illegal for a person seeking legal assistance from him; (2) agree to do what a person seeking legal assistance from him asks him where he: (a) is personally involved in the subject matter of an agreement with a client and is in a conflict of interest with the person; (b) was involved in the case as a judge, umpire or arbitrator, mediator, procurator, investigator, investigative inquiry officer, expert, specialist or interpreter, is an injured party or witness in the case, or if he was an official empowered to make a decision in favor of the person; (c) is related by blood or marriage to an official who was or is involved in an investigation or hearing of the person's case; or (d) renders legal assistance to a client whose interests are at variance with those of the person; (3) act in a case against the wishes of a client, except where the lawyer is convinced that the client has given a false confession; (4) state publicly that a client's guilt has been proven if the client denies it; (5) breach legal professional privilege; or (6) withdraw from representation.

An attorney is forbidden from colluding with the police.

An attorney is required to: (1) honestly, reasonably and in good faith uphold the rights and legitimate interests of a client using all means; (2) comply with the statutory requirements for a lawyer's involvement in criminal proceedings as a counsel for the defense when appointed by investigative inquiry authorities, preliminary investigation authorities or a court, as well as rendering legal assistance; (3) continually improve his knowledge and qualifications; (4) comply with the code of ethics of the legal profession and the decisions made by authorities of the bar association of the Russian Federation; and (5) pay each month, from fees received, contributions to the general expenses of the bar association.

III. Organizations of Attorneys

37. Attorney practice takes the following forms: sole attorney proprietorship, attorney association, law firm and legal clinic. An attorney has discretion to choose the form of attorney practice and notify the chosen form and location of attorney practice to the bar council.

Having formed a sole attorney proprietorship, the attorney sends the bar council a notice by registered letter specifying his details, the location and contact information for telephone, postal and other communications between the bar council and the attorney. A sole attorney proprietorship is not a legal entity.

Two or more lawyers are entitled to form an attorney association. An attorney association is a not-for-profit organization based on membership and operating under its charter, established by its incorporators, and the preincorporation contract made by them. An attorney association can be incorporated by attorneys whose details are entered in one state register only.

Two or more attorneys are entitled to form a law firm. The lawyers forming a law firm enter into a partnership agreement in writing. Under the partnership agreement, the partner lawyers undertake to pool their efforts to provide legal assistance on behalf of all partners. The law firm is managed by the managing partner, unless otherwise provided for in the partnership agreement. A legal services agreement with a client is made by the managing partner or another partner on behalf of all partners based on the powers of attorney granted by them. The powers of attorney list all limits of the remit of the partner entering into agreements and transactions with clients and third parties. Clients and third parties are notified of these limits. A law firm may not transform into a business or any other not-for-profit organization.

Where the total number of lawyers in all legal practices in a judicial district is fewer than two per federal judge, the bar association establishes a legal clinic. The legal clinic is a not-for-profit organization.

38. A bar association is a nongovernmental not-for-profit organization based on compulsory membership of attorneys. It could be that there is only one bar association in a "subject" (state) of the Russian Federation. The supreme authority of the bar association is the meeting of lawyers. In a bar association with more than 300 members, the supreme bar authority is the conference of lawyers. A meeting (conference) of lawyers is convened no less frequently than once a year.

The jurisdiction of the meeting (conference) of attorneys includes: (1) formation of the bar council, including the election of new council members and removal of council members; (2) election of the audit commission members and election of qualifications commission members from among the lawyers; (3) determination of the amount of obligatory contributions from lawyers to the general expenses of the bar association; (4) approval of the bar association's upkeep budget; (5) approval of the audit commission's report on the findings of an audit of the bar association's finances and operations.

The bar association's assets are formed through contributions made by attorneys, grants and charitable aid (donations).

Chapter 3. The Bailiffs

39. The execution of the judgment is carried out by the court and bailiff service. In Russia, a big reform was initiated in 1997 when the Federal Bailiff Service was established. It became a part of the system of agencies of the Ministry of Justice. The territorial bodies are located in every region of the Russian Federation.

The bailiffs carry out not only the execution of the court's judgments but also of other acts (e.g., decisions on administrative offenses). Bailiffs also ensure the safety of judges and other participants during the proceedings.

The Director of the Federal Bailiff Service is appointed by the President of the Russian Federation. The Federal Bailiff Service has been a member of the International Union of Judicial Officers since 2015. In order to become a bailiff a person must be a citizen of Russia and be at least 21 years old. There are no requirements concerning a university degree in law. Before presenting an applicant for the bailiff's position, there is a preliminary coordination of the candidacy with a medical commission.

Part II. Jurisdiction

Chapter 1. Domestic Jurisdiction

§1. Subject Matter Jurisdiction

40. In Russia, general courts and arbitrazh (commercial) courts specialize in a particular area of the law. Russian legislation gives jurisdiction over some types of cases to arbitrazh courts only.

As a general rule, arbitrazh (commercial) courts consider economic disputes and other cases related to the exercise of entrepreneurial activities. Additional criteria are the parties. They are legal entities or individuals that have the status of an individual entrepreneur. There is also special jurisdiction of arbitrazh courts: (1) insolvency (bankruptcy); (2) denial of registration or evasion of registration by legal entities; (3) disputes arising from the activities of depositaries; (4) protection of intellectual property rights; and (5) protection of business reputation.

Courts of general jurisdiction consider civil disputes, labor and employment disputes, family law and consumer protection cases as well as other types of cases.

§2. Venue (Territorial Jurisdiction)

41. There are several types of jurisdiction. As a general rule, a claim is filed with a court at the location of the defendant. At the same time the plaintiff has a choice of jurisdiction. A claim against the defendant whose location is unknown may be filed with the court of location of his property or at the last known place of his residence. A claim against an organization resulting from the activity of its affiliate or representation may also be instituted in court at the place of location of its affiliate or representation. Claims on the exaction of alimony and on the establishment of paternity may also be instituted at the place of residence of the plaintiff. Claims for the dissolution of a marriage may also be instituted at the place of residence of the plaintiff. Claims for the recompense of the damage caused by severe injury and other kinds of damage to the health or as a result of the death of the breadwinner may also be instituted by the plaintiff in court at the place of his residence or at the place of inflicting damage. Claims for the restoration of the labor, pension and housing rights, for the return of the property or of the cost involved in the recompense of the losses inflicted upon a citizen by an unlawful conviction, by an unlawful bringing to criminal responsibility or by an unlawful application as a measure of restraint of taking into custody or of the recognizance not to leave, or by an unlawful imposition of an administrative punishment in the form of arrest, may also be instituted in the court at the place of the plaintiff's residence. Claims for the protection of consumers rights may also be instituted in court at the place of the plaintiff's residence or stay, or at the place of the conclusion or of the execution of the contract. Claims for the recompense of the losses caused by the collision of ships, for recovery of wages and other sums of money which are due to members of the ship's crew for their work aboard the ship, of the outlays on repatriation and contributions for social insurance, for recovery of remuneration for rendering help and rescue at sea may be also instituted in court at the location of the defendant's ship or of the port of the ship's registration. Claims stemming from contracts in which the place of their execution is pointed out may also be instituted in the court at the place of execution of such contract.

42. There is exclusive jurisdiction. Claims for rights to land plots, buildings, residential and nonresidential quarters, as well as for relieving the property from seizure are filed with the court at the place of location of these objects or the seized property. Claims of the creditors of the legator instituted before the bequest is accepted by the heirs are cognizable to the court at the place of the opening of the inheritance. Claims against shippers stemming from contracts of shipment are filed in court at the place of location of the shipper against whom the claim was filed in the established order.

There is jurisdiction of several interconnected cases. A claim against several defendants residing or staying at different places is instituted in the court at the place of residence or at the place of stay of one of the defendants at the plaintiff's choice. A counterclaim is filed with the court at the place of consideration of the initial claim. A civil claim stemming from a criminal case—unless it was instituted or resolved in the proceedings on the criminal case—is presented for consideration by way of the civil legal procedure.

There is agreed jurisdiction. The parties may agree between themselves to alter the territorial jurisdiction of the given case before it is taken over by the court for its proceedings.

§3. Resolution of Jurisdiction Conflicts

43. The Civil Procedural Code establishes a special procedure for handing over a case taken over by the court for its proceedings to another court. A case taken over by the court for its proceedings with the observation of the rules for jurisdiction is resolved by it on the merits, even though subsequently it will become cognizable to another court. The court hands over the case for consideration to another court if: (1) a defendant whose place of residence or place of stay was not earlier known has filed a petition for handing over the case to the court at the place of his residence or stay; (2) both parties have filed a petition for the consideration of the case at the place of location of most of the evidence; (3) during the consideration of the case in the given court it has transpired that it was taken over for the proceedings with a violation of the rules for jurisdiction; or (4) after the disqualification of one or several judges or for other reasons, the replacement of judges or the consideration of the case in the given court has become impossible. Under these circumstances the transfer of the case will be effected by the higher placed court. On handing over the case to another court or on the refusal to hand over the case to another court a ruling of the court against which a special complaint may be lodged will be issued. The transfer of the case to another court will be effected after the expiration of the time term for filing an appeal against this ruling, and if a complaint is lodged—after a court ruling is issued on leaving the complaint without satisfaction. A case sent over from one court to another will be accepted for consideration by the court to which it is forwarded.

Disputes on the jurisdiction between the courts in the Russian Federation are inadmissible.

In addition to the legal issue in dispute, the subject matter jurisdiction of a court may be determined by the amount of money involved in the dispute or the monetary value of the dispute.

Part III. Actions and Proceedings

44. There are several stages of the court proceedings.

Chapter 1. Proceedings in First Instance

§1. The Institution of a Civil Case

45. The institution of a civil case in court can be carried out by submission of a claim, complaint or statement. It could be submitted either in paper or in electronic form, but only in arbitrazh courts. The judge decides on the initiation of proceedings in a case within five days from the moment of receipt of the claim, but it is not bound by this time limit. The judge issues a ruling by which the civil case is instituted in the Court of First Instance. Generally, all the necessary steps for the acceptance of the claim and institution of a civil case have to be taken on the same day the plaintiff appealed to the court.

When accepting the claim the judge has to check whether the person concerned has the right to an appeal to the court for judicial protection and whether it is carried out according to a certain due process. The conditions for the initiation of the proceedings are:

(1) following a pretrial dispute resolution procedure by the plaintiff;
(2) jurisdiction over the subject matter to a particular court;
(3) procedural capacity of the plaintiff;
(4) having the authorities for the administration of the case;
(5) following the requirement of a written form of the claim;
(6) payment of the state tax.

If any of these conditions is missing, the judge has either to return the claim, or to refuse its acceptance, or to leave the claim without progress. If all formal requirements are presented, the judge should issue a ruling of accepting a claim and starts a preparation stage.

§2. Preparation for the Trial

46. The institution of a civil case is followed by the second stage—preparation for the trial. The purpose of this stage is to provide the prompt and correct adjudication of the case within one court session, to eliminate the judicial red tape and bureaucracy in legal proceedings. This stage consists of the following procedural actions.

The plaintiff transfers to the respondent a copy of the evidence and files motions for the discovery of the evidence if it cannot be received without the aid of the court.

The respondent can clarify the claim and the actual grounds of the claim with the plaintiff, present the objections to the claim before the plaintiff and the court, transfer the evidence that proves the objections and file motions for the discovery of the evidence if it cannot be received without the aid of the court.

47. During the preparation stage the judge:

- guides the proceedings and explains to the parties their procedural rights and duties;
- examines the plaintiff or his attorney on the claim and offers to introduce the additional evidence, if necessary;
- examines the respondent on the circumstances of the case, determines whether there are objections against the claim and what the basis is for the objections;
- resolves an issue of the co-plaintiffs, co-defendants and the third parties joining the proceedings, an issue of the replacement of an improper defendant, or an issue of joinder or separation of separate claims;
- takes measures to reconcile the parties, to reach the settlement agreements and explains to them the right to apply to the arbitration court for dispute settlement;
- informs the persons and the organizations concerned on the time and the place of the trial;
- resolves an issue of the summon of witnesses;
- commissions an expert assessment and the experts;
- resolves an issue of subpoena to appear as an expert or a translator;
- discovers the evidence which parties cannot receive independently on request of the parties and persons participating in the case and other persons participating in the case;
- makes view of the premises;
- takes provisional measures application; and
- appoints the preliminary court session.

§3. Trial

48. The third stage is the trial. In this stage consideration of the merits takes place and usually it ends with adjudication. Trials consist of four parts: (1) preparatory part; (2) consideration of the case on the merits; (3) judicial pleadings; and (4) adjudication and announcement of the decision. All of them, having a certain independence, are closely connected and consistently follow each other.

The task of the court in the preparatory part is to examine whether there are necessary conditions for the trial in the particular court session. For this purpose the court has to resolve three issues: (1) whether consideration of the case is possible with the particular composition of the court; (2) whether hearing of the case is possible if any of the persons participating in the case are not present during the court session; and (3) whether consideration of the case is possible with the present evidence.

At a certain time the chairman opens the court session and announces which case is subject to consideration. Then the court session secretary reports who from the persons summoned before the court is present, whether absent participants were informed about the case hearing and what the reasons for their absence are. In practice, these procedural actions are quite often made by the chairman himself.

The witnesses present leave the courtroom prior to their interrogation. It is explained to them that they will be recalled into the courtroom for testifying. The chairman ensures measures so that the witnesses interrogated cannot communicate with others not interrogated.

49. The chairman announces the composition of the court—the prosecutor for the case, the attorneys of the parties, the third parties, the expert, the specialist, the translator, the court session secretary—and explains their right to self-recusals and recusals. The judge, the prosecutor, the court session secretary, the expert, the specialist and the translator cannot participate in the trial and are subject to recusal if they have a personal, direct or indirect interest in the outcome of the case or if there are other circumstances raising doubts as to their impartiality. The judge cannot hear the case if: (1) in the previous consideration of the same case he participated as a prosecutor, attorney, witness, expert, specialist, translator, court session secretary; (2) he is the relative of any participant in the case, or their attorney; or (3) he has a personal, direct or indirect interest in the outcome of the case or if there are other circumstances raising doubts as to the objectivity and impartiality of the judge.

The chairman asks whether the participants have any motions or statements. If there are any statements or motions on evidence discovery or on other issues connected with the case trial, the court is obliged to hear the opinion of other participants in the case. The statements and motions are resolved by issuing a court ruling, by which the motions are granted or dismissed. These rulings have to be reasoned. The judge is obliged to announce the issued ruling immediately.

The second part of the trial—consideration of the case on the merits—begins with the report of the chairman. In the report, the judge has to state briefly: (1) who the plaintiff is, who the respondent is and what the grounds for the claim are; (2) whether there are written objections of the respondent and what their essence is; and (3) all the evidence available in the case.

50. All administrative actions made by the parties in the courtroom have to be recorded accurately. The plaintiff's statement of renunciation of the suit, recognition of the claim by the respondent or the conditions of the settlement agreement of the parties have to be placed on record and signed, respectively, by the plaintiff, the respondent or both parties. If the administrative actions mentioned are expressed in the written statements addressed to the court, these statements have to be added to the case materials and placed on record.

For the sake of ascertaining to the fullest extent possible the facts and circumstances, the persons participating in the case are granted the right to ask each other questions. The questions are set with the permission of the chairman, who has to ensure that the questions concern the merits of the considered case. The judge rejects the questions which do not concern the merits of the considered case.

51. Having heard and having announced the explanations of the persons participating in the case, the court has to establish the sequence of further evidence discovery, an order of interrogation of witnesses, experts and the order of discovery of other evidence. The court resolves this issue, having listened to the opinions of the persons present and participating in the case. Most often, the court begins the evidence discovery with the interrogation of witnesses. Each witness is interrogated separately. The chairman, having revealed the relation of the witness to the persons participating in the case, invites the witness to report everything that he or she knows personally that relates to the case. The witness testifies in a free form about the circumstances he or she knows. After the testimony the witness can be asked questions. The party and the party's attorney who called for the witness ask first, and then the other persons participating in the case and their attorneys may ask their questions. The witness called at the initiative of the court is asked by the plaintiff first. Judges can ask the witness questions at any time. At the interrogation of witnesses under the age of 14 and witnesses between the ages of 14 and 6 by court order their teacher will be called. In case of need parents, adoptive parents, trustees or curator are called. The mentioned persons can ask questions of the witness with the permission of the chairman.

For the sake of the protection of personal correspondence, written evidence can be revealed (announced) and investigated in a public hearing only with the consent of the person who is the author of the correspondence. Otherwise a private hearing will take place and the court will issue a special ruling.

52. The court examines the material evidence, and it is shown to the persons participating in the case.

Unlike the former Civil Procedure Code of 1964, the new Code allows examination of audio or video recordings during the court session.

After the examination of all the evidence the chairman gives the floor to the prosecutor. The prosecutor draws general conclusions on the merits of the case. The prosecutor has to:

- briefly state the public importance of the considered case;
- analyze in detail the examined evidence and specify which evidence can be considered reliable;
- state which facts were established in court and which should be considered unspecified.

53. To conclude, the prosecutor is obliged to refer to the legal norms that have to be applied in the consideration of the case, and to specify how in his opinion the case needs to be adjudicated based on the presented norms.

After the conclusions of the prosecutor, the judge asks the parties to the case or their attorneys whether they wish to present additional explanations. In the absence of such statements, the chairman announces the consideration of the case on the merits to be completed, and the case passes to the judicial pleadings.

The next part of the court proceedings—the judicial pleadings—aims at summing up the results of the examination of the evidence. The persons participating in the case state and give reasons for their conclusions about which evidence should be considered reliable, which facts of the case should be considered established and which unspecified, what the content of the dispute is, which law should be applied and how the case should be adjudicated.

The judicial pleadings consist of the statements of the parties to the case and their attorneys. In the judicial pleadings the plaintiff and his attorney come first, then come the respondent and his attorney. Following the statements of all participants in the judicial pleadings, they can make remarks regarding their statements. The right of giving the final remarks always belongs to the respondent and his attorney. The participants in the judicial pleadings have no right to refer to circumstances that were not investigated in the court session, nor to refer to the evidence that was investigated. After the judicial pleadings the chairman announces that the court will retire to chambers to consider its decision.

§4. Judgment

54. The next part of the trial is the delivery and announcement of the decision. During the discussion and the delivery of a decision only the judges who are part of the composition of the court for the case are allowed in chambers. The presence of other persons in chambers is not allowed. Such order creates the conditions for excluding additional pressure on the judges during adjudication. Violation of the secrecy of meetings of judges is the unconditional grounds for the reversal of judgment. All the issues arising during the trial are resolved by the means of majority voting. When considering each issue, none of the judges has the right to abstain from voting. A judge not in agreement with the solution of the majority can state a dissenting opinion, which is added to the case material.

In chambers, the judges have to analyze and evaluate the seized evidence based on comprehensive, complete and objective examination of all the facts of the case presented in the court session, being guided only by the law and their sense of justice.

The court adjudicates the case based on the requirements declared by the plaintiff. However, in some cases provided by law, the court can go beyond the declared requirements. The court is obliged to deliver the decision immediately after the trial. When dealing with a particularly difficult case the delivery of the reasoned decision can be postponed up to five days, but in this situation the operative part of the decision has to be announced in the same court session that the case trial ended. After signing the decision the judges return to the courtroom where the chairman announces the decision.

55. The structure and contents of the decision are regulated by the Civil Procedural Code. This consists of four parts stated in strict sequence: the introductory part, the descriptive part, the rationale for the judgment and the operative part.

The introductory part has to contain the time period taken for adjudication, the place of adjudication, which is defined by the location of the court hearing for the case, and the name of the court that delivered the decision as well as the court's composition.

The descriptive part of the decision has to contain the requirements stated in the claim, and the circumstances confirming the requirements. It reflects the respondent's position. If there are objections from the respondent, the reasons for the claim's nonrecognition are stated briefly.

The rationale for the judgment has to contain the actual and legal justifications for the court's conclusions. It also contains the facts of the case established by the court, the evidence on which the conclusions are based, the argumentation for the court's rejection of the evidence if so determined and the laws on which the decision is based.

In the operative part of the decision, the results of the judicial proceedings are presented in a concise and final manner: a conclusion about the satisfaction of the claim or the dismissal of the claim in full or in part. The operative part clarifies what the court has decided on each issue separately and on the counterclaim, which of the parties enjoys the challenged right, and what actions need to be taken by the liable person.

56. Generally, the trial of a civil case ends with the decision. But in some cases it ends without it. There are two forms of the termination of proceedings without a decision: discontinuance of proceedings and leaving the claim without consideration.

These forms differ both in terms of the grounds and in terms of the legal consequences of them. The discontinuance of proceedings generally takes place when the plaintiff does not have the right to judicial protection. Therefore, the discontinuance of proceedings excludes the possibility of instituting a second proceeding for the same case. Leaving the claim without consideration may occur when the plaintiff or the applicant has the right to judicial protection but the conditions of its realization were not met. In the case of leaving the claim without consideration the plaintiff or the applicant does not lose the right to initiate identical proceedings in court again after the elimination of the defects.

§5. Default Proceedings

57. If a defendant duly notified about the time and the place of the court session who has not reported about the valid reasons for his failure to appear and who has not requested to consider the case in his absence does not come to the court session, the case may be considered by way of default proceedings. The court shall issue a ruling on the consideration of a case in accordance with such procedure.

A copy of the court decision shall be sent to the defendant not later than three days as from the day of its adoption. The plaintiff has the right to file an application for cancellation of this court decision with the court that has adopted the decision. Such application must be filed within seven days as from the day on which a copy of the decision was handed to the applicant. A court decision may likewise be appealed by the parties in the appellate procedure within a month after the expiry of the time period for the filing by the defendant of an application for cancellation of this court decision or, if such application has been filed, within a month as from the date on which the court has rejected the application. If the court decision is cancelled, the court shall resume the consideration of the case on merit.

Chapter 2. Review Proceedings

§1. General

58. A court decision may contain errors or simply be unjust or even illegal. The right to appeal and review judgments is one of the basic rights that is recognized by most procedural systems. Appellate review is the opportunity for the parties to try to correct an injustice that may be contained in a judgment. Two different systems of review are widespread in the world. Which one is used depends on the kind of judicial errors that are considered by a court of the review instance: errors of fact or errors of law.

The Russian system of review is influenced by continental European legislation, especially by French and German law. Such legislation provides for appellate and cassational procedures. However, uniquely, the Russian system also provides for supervisory proceedings. Russian review proceedings are divided into four categories:

(1) appeal;
(2) cassation;
(3) supervisory proceedings; and
(4) an appeal founded on new or newly discovered facts.

§2. Appeal

59. The decisions of a Court of First Instance that have not yet entered into force may be appealed through the appeals procedure. The appellate court rehears the case with full authority to review all the circumstances in the case. The court will assess all evidence presented in the first instance, as well as any new evidence. Cases in a court of an appellate instance are examined by panels of judges and not by a single judge. An appeal has to be filed within one month of the date on which a Court of First Instance issued the decision in its final form.

§3. Cassation

60. A court of cassation is not entitled to consider matters if they were not established by a Court of First Instance. It does not review the circumstances of the case and does not admit new evidence, rather the court will only consider the correct application of material and procedural law and the legal reasoning behind the application. Nor can it rule on the credibility of evidence. Parties to the case cannot ask the court to consider new evidence; they can only present the evidence that was examined by the Court of First Instance. It is required to base the factual deliberations on the facts as established by a Court of First Instance. A court of cassation can also remit a case for retrial.

§4. Supervisory Proceedings

61. After the cassation process, a supervisory appeal may potentially be filed. A supervisory procedure is an exceptional feature of Russian civil procedure. Review by way of supervision is a special procedure that allows additional reexamination of judgments which have already entered into legal force. It stems from legislation of the Russian Empire of the seventeenth, eighteenth and nineteenth centuries.

During the Soviet period, the right to apply to a supervisory court belonged only to a limited number of officials, such as chief judges and their deputies and the Procurator General and his deputies. Parties to a case did not have such right. In 1980, 8,618 decisions were revoked by way of supervision. In contrast, 12,500 were revoked by way of supervision in 1989.

62. In modern Russia, review by way of supervision is regulated in a different manner. It is stipulated in the Constitution and in the new 2003 Civil Procedural Code. It exists in addition to the appeal and cassation instances and allows for the reexamination of judgments which have already entered into legal force and which may have already been decided under a cassational appeal. The right to apply to the court of supervision belongs only to the parties to the case and any other persons whose rights were abused by the judgment. Appeals via supervision may only be considered by the Presidium of the Supreme Court, by military assembly of the Supreme Court, by judicial tribunal of the Supreme Court for civil cases, by presidium of a military court, and by Presidium of the Supreme Court of a "subject" (state) within the Federation. It is possible to appeal to a court of supervision within three months of the date on which a judgment enters into legal force.

When reviewing a case by way of supervision, the court considers only questions of law on the basis of materials available in the case. Although the supervisory instance may refuse to accept lower courts' findings of fact, it has no power to establish new facts or to consider new evidence. As a general rule, the court verifies the correctness of the application and interpretation of provisions of material law and norms of procedural law by the courts of the first and cassational instances only within the limits of the arguments contained in the appeal. However, in the interest of legality, the higher court may also go beyond the limits of the appeal. The court of the supervisory instance may render a new judgment when it is not necessary to consider additional facts or evidence. Some 300,000 appeals a year are considered by the courts of general jurisdiction by way of supervision. In 1996, 15,215 decisions were cancelled in the supervisory instance and 20,270 in 2002. That is one-third of all annulled decisions. In contrast 17,482 decisions were annulled in the supervisory instance in 2004 (after the adoption of the new Civil Procedural Code). That is 20% of all annulled decisions.

63. The possibility of reexamining a judgment which has already entered into legal force is a moot point. Does this conflict with the principle of res judicata? There are two points of view. Some scholars believe that the supervisory instance is an additional opportunity to correct the decision and rectify judicial errors.[16] Others emphasize that it conflicts with the principle of res judicata.[17] The position of the European Court of Human Rights is interesting in this context. In *Ryabykh v. Russia*, No. 52854/99 dated July 24, 2003, it simultaneously maintains two different positions on the Russian supervisory instance. On the one hand, it believes that review by way of supervision conflicts with the principle of res judicata (Articles 52, 55–57 of *Ryabykh v. Russia*, Article 25 of *Pravednaya v. Russia*). On the other hand, it does not conflict with it because it is used to rectify judicial errors (Articles 25, 28 *Pravednaya v. Russia*, Article 52 of *Ryabykh v. Russia*).

Meanwhile, Russian supervisory procedure was reformed in 2010 and the right to appeal was limited to a strict number of cases. Nowadays, the supervisory appeal is the exception to the rule.

§5. Appeal Founded on New or Newly Discovered Facts

64. An appeal due to newly discovered facts is one of the ways of legal examination of the consideration of the case. Newly discovered facts are the facts that existed at the time of the consideration of the case and that are of significance for the correct adjudication of which the applicant or the court had no, and could not have had any, knowledge. The main objective of the court is to determine the existence or absence of newly discovered facts and to establish whether they affected the decision issued.

The decisions that have entered into legal force, court rulings of the first instance court and of the justice of the peace can only be the object of revision on newly discovered facts. The revision is carried out by the court that delivered the decision.

The grounds for the revision of decisions due to newly discovered facts are the following:

(1) circumstances significant for the case, of which the applicant had no and could not have had any knowledge;
(2) falsification of evidence, deliberately false expert opinion, deliberately false witness testimony, deliberately incorrect translation that resulted in the delivery of an unlawful or an unsubstantiated decision on a given case and established by an effective court sentence;
(3) criminal deeds of a person participating in the case or of his attorney, or criminal deeds of a judge, committed during the consideration of the given case and established by an effective court sentence.

Having considered the application, the court either satisfies it and reverses the decision, or refuses the revision. In case of reversal, the case is considered on the merits in the general proceedings.

16. Терехова Л.А., Надзорное производство в гражданском процессе. М., 2009 (Lidya Terelhova, Supervisory Procedure in Civil Proceedings, 2007).
17. Ефимов А.Е., Надзорное производство в арбитражном процессе. М., 2008 (Alexey Efimov, Supervisory Procedure in Commercial Proceedings, 2008).

Part IV. Legal Costs and Legal Aid

65. Payment of a duty to the state for use of the courts was introduced in 1930 and has been maintained ever since. There is no special theory on costs in Russian doctrine in respect of civil procedure. However, the purpose of court costs and fines is not only to reimburse the state for expenses, but also to prevent groundless cases from being brought.

Individuals and companies have to fund litigation from their own resources. There is no ban on obtaining loans from banks or other lenders, nor on attorneys paying the state duty for clients. Legal Expenses Insurance or after-the-event insurance for individuals or companies is not applicable under Russian legislation.

In general, free legal aid is not available under Russian legislation. However, there are some exceptions. Members of the Colleges of Advocates are supposed to give free legal advice in some cases.

66. Legislation provides that legal aid will be rendered free of charge to, first, citizens of the Russian Federation whose families have an average per capita annual income that is lower than the value of the minimum subsistence level established by law and to, second, citizens of the Russian Federation living alone whose incomes are lower than the value established by law, in the following cases:

- to plaintiffs in cases concerning alimony, damage relating to a breadwinner's death, maiming or other job-related injury to health;
- to veterans of World War II: on issues not relating to entrepreneurial activity;
- to citizens of the Russian Federation when applications for pensions and benefits are drawn up;
- to citizens of the Russian Federation who have suffered from political repression on issues relating to rehabilitation.

A person who is granted legal aid is not required to pay the state duty and expenses. Instead, such costs are to be paid by the defendant if he loses. If both parties are relieved from payment of the state duty and expenses, the losses should be compensated for from the funds of the federal budget.

In all cases legal assistance will be rendered free of charge to minors who reside in official institutions for preventing child neglect and offenses committed by minors.

Those filing a claim with a court will pay the state duty. The amount depends on the type of court, type of claim and amount of claim. Claimants usually engage their own translators if they need translation services. Service of process, enforcement of a judgment and assistance of a bailiff are free of charge.

67. There are two systems of courts in Russia that hear civil cases. Courts of general jurisdiction hear normal civil cases involving individuals. State arbitration courts hear commercial civil cases involving legal entities. The state duty for filing a claim with a court of general jurisdiction ranges from 4% for small claims to 0.5% for other claims. Some categories of plaintiffs are relieved from paying this state duty mainly due to social reasons.

In addition to the state duty, the Civil Procedural Code defines "court charges" as:

(1) sums to be paid to witnesses, experts, specialists and interpreters;
(2) expenses relating to remuneration for the services of an interpreter incurred by foreign citizens and by stateless persons, unless otherwise stipulated in an international treaty to which the Russian Federation is a signatory state;
(3) expenses on the fares and accommodations of third parties made in connection with summons to court;
(4) fees for the services of the attorneys;
(5) expenses for carrying out an examination of evidence;
(6) compensation for actual loss of time by the party;
(7) postal expenses;
(8) other expenses recognized by the court as necessary.

The state duty is to be paid by the applicant when filing a claim with the court. If it is not paid, the codes provide for the court to discontinue the claim. Where a claimant is relieved from paying the state duty, it has to be paid by the loser at the end of the case, pro rata to the claim being satisfied. Where a claim has been partially satisfied and the respondent has been relieved from paying the state duty, the state duty is to be levied on the claimant.

68. At the time of filing an application for a witness, expert or specialist to be involved, the party applying for their involvement must deposit the relevant sum in the special bank account of the Judicial Department to cover their costs or such other charges as are recognized by the court as necessary. Where both parties have made the same application, the amount should be deposited in equal parts. No "legal aid" covers such costs. Where the involvement of the witness, expert or specialist has been initiated by the court, the relevant amount should be paid by the state. Translation charges will be paid by the state upon the translators' performance of their duties, except where the parties engage translators themselves.

The party considered to be the loser according to the decision issued by the court has to reimburse the winner the amount of the "court charges" paid, as defined above. Where the claim has been partially satisfied, the loser has to reimburse the court charges pro rata to the amount of the satisfied claim.

If the state grants "legal aid" to a party, this only exempts payment of state duty and expenses. The lawyer is not paid by the state, and the party must either agree to pay the lawyer (in civil cases—the party does not pay in criminal cases) or the lawyer must agree to act for free. There is no special tariff for fee shifting.

Lawyers are free to negotiate their fees with their client. The level of fees charged depends on the lawyer's qualifications. An agreement involving a "success fee" is not enforceable in Russian courts against clients, because the Russian Constitutional Court has ruled that a success fee could negatively influence proceedings, but clients usually do not refuse to pay an agreed success fee because they have a longstanding relationship with their lawyers.

Part V. Evidence

Chapter 1. Burden of Proof and Admissibility of Evidence

69. Evidence is determined by the Civil Procedural Code as the information obtained in the legally stipulated order about the facts on whose grounds the court establishes the existence or absence of the facts substantiating the claims and objections of the parties, as well as of other circumstances that are of importance for the correct consideration and resolution of the case. This information may be obtained from the explanations of the parties and third persons, from the testimony of witnesses, from written and material evidence, from audio and video recordings, and from expert conclusions. Evidence obtained by violation of the law will have no legal force, and the decision of the court cannot be based on it.

Each party will prove those facts to which it refers as to the grounds for its claims and objections, unless otherwise stipulated in federal law. The court will determine which facts are of importance for the case and which party is obliged to prove them, and will submit these facts for discussion, even if the parties have not referred to some of them.

The evidence will be supplied by the parties. The court has the right to suggest that they supply additional evidence. There is an important rule that if it is difficult for the parties to supply the necessary evidence, the court will render them assistance at their petition in the collection and the reclamation of evidence. This means that the court is passive as a general rule, but it becomes active if there is a petition by a party. In the petition for the reclamation of evidence, the evidence will be designated and so will which particular facts of importance for the correct consideration and resolution of the case may be confirmed or refuted by this evidence. The reasons for interfering with the receipt of the evidence should also be indicated.

70. The court may examine and investigate the written or material evidence at the place of its location if it is impossible or difficult to bring the evidence to the court. The court will accept only that evidence which is of importance for the consideration and resolution of the case. The facts recognized by the court as generally known will not require proving. The circumstances established by the court decision on an earlier considered case, which has entered into legal force, are obligatory for the court. These facts will not be proved again and will not be subject to dispute when considering another case in which the same persons are taking part.

The court will assess the evidence in accordance with its inherent conviction, based on an all-round, complete, objective and direct investigation of the evidence contained in the case. No kind of evidence will have, for the court, its force established in advance. The court will assess the referability, admissibility and authenticity of each piece of evidence separately, as well as the sufficiency and the interconnection of the evidence in the aggregate. The court is obliged to reflect the results of the assessment of evidence in the decision in which the motives will be cited because of which some evidence is accepted as the means for substantiating the conclusions of the court, while other evidence is rejected by the court, as well as the grounds on which some evidence is preferred to other evidence.

Chapter 2. Administration of Evidence

§1. General

71. The court cannot decide a case without determining the factual circumstances. For determining them it uses evidence. The aim of the court is to protect rights and interests foreseen by law. To protect these rights, the court has to determine whether the right that a plaintiff demands to be protected really exists or not and whether the corresponding obligation is imposed on a defendant and how it is expressed. Evidence is means of proof, by use of which the court can establish factual circumstances for deciding the case correctly.

As far as the components of modern Russian evidence law are concerned, they are based on practically the same approaches as the ones in the 1864 Civil Procedural Code: the decisions of the courts are binding for each other (prejudicial nature of judicial acts); the subject of proof consists of explanations and objections of the parties; there are facts not subject to proof (well-known and presumed facts); allocation of obligations on proof, etc.[18]

The Civil Procedural Code defines the kinds of evidence: explanations of parties (the third person), testimony of witnesses, written and material evidence, expert opinion and materials giving statements of facts.

§2. Explanations of the Parties

72. Explanations of the parties are an independent and important source of evidence. They should concern the facts known to the parties which are of importance for the correct consideration of the case. If the party obliged to prove its claims or objections holds back the evidence at its disposal and does not present it to the court, the court has the right to base its conclusions on the explanations of the other party. The acknowledgment by a party of the circumstances on which the other party bases its claims or objections relieves the latter from the need to further prove these facts. The acknowledgment will be entered into the record of the court session. The acknowledgment stated in a written application will be enclosed with the case materials.

§3. Witness Testimony

73. Witnesses make a necessary and valuable contribution to the civil justice system by giving evidence in court. A witness is a person who may dispose of certain information about the facts which is of importance for the consideration and the resolution of the case. Information supplied by a witness will not be seen as proof if he cannot name the source of his knowledge. A person requesting to summon a witness

18. Irina Reshetnikova, *Judicial Reforms in Russia: 1864 to 2014*, 3(2) Russian L.J. 114 (2015).

is obliged to indicate what particular facts of importance for the consideration and the resolution of the case the witness can confirm.

The following persons will not be interrogated as witnesses: (1) attorneys, about the circumstances that they have learned as the attorney; (2) judges, about the questions which have arisen in the retiring room (chambers) in connection with the discussion of the circumstances of the case when passing the court decision; and (3) priests of religious organizations, about circumstances which have become known to them from confession. The following persons have the right to refuse to give evidence as a witness: (1) the person, against himself; (2) a spouse, against the other spouse, children, and the parents, against their children; (3) the brothers and sisters, against one another, the grandmother and the grandfather, against their grandchildren, and the grandchildren, against their grandfather and grandmother; and (4) the deputies of the legislative bodies in respect of information which has become known to them in connection with the discharge of their authorized, official powers.

The person summoned as a witness is obliged to appear in court at the appointed time and to give truthful evidence. The witness may be interrogated by the court at the place of his stay if he is in no condition to come to the court summons because of illness, old age, invalidity and other valid reasons. The witness will bear criminal responsibility for giving false evidence and for refusal to give evidence on motives not envisioned by law.

§4. Written and Material Evidence

74. Written evidence should be introduced to the court in the form of documents. It could be the acts, agreements, reference notes, business correspondence and other documents and materials made out in the form of digital or graphic recordings, including those obtained through the use of facsimile, electronic or other communication devices or by another method allowing to ascertain the authenticity of the document which contains information on the circumstances of importance for the consideration and for the resolution of the case. Written evidence will be presented in its original form or in the form of a copy. A document obtained in a foreign state will be recognized as written evidence in court if it is legalized in the established order.

Tangible evidence are the objects which in their external appearance, properties and place of location or because of their other features may serve as a means for the establishment of circumstances of importance for the consideration and resolution of a case.

Audio and video recordings also could be used in court as evidence. A person who has submitted audio or video recordings on an electronic or another kind of device, or who has filed a petition for their supply on demand, is obliged to point out when, by whom and under what conditions these recordings were made.

§5. Expert Evidence

75. Expert opinion is one of the most important forms of evidence. If questions arise during the consideration of the case which require special knowledge in various fields of science, technology, the arts and the handicrafts, the court should appoint an expert on the subject. The parties may only petition the court to ask questions; they do not have right to appoint experts. The performance of the appointment may be entrusted to a legal expert agency, to a particular expert or to several experts. Each of the parties has the right to put to the court questions which are subject to resolution by the expert(s) in carrying out the appointment and arriving at an opinion. The final circle of questions on which the conclusions of an expert is required will be delineated by the court. The court is obliged to motivate a deviation from the suggested questions. The parties and the other persons taking part in the case have the right to request the court appoint the performance of this task to a particular legal expert agency or to entrust it to a particular expert; to disqualify an expert; to formulate questions for the expert(s) to resolve; to get acquainted with the court ruling on the appointment of an expert and with the questions formulated; to become acquainted with the expert conclusion; to file a petition to the court for the appointment of a repeated, additional or complex expert opinion undertaking, or of a commission which will undertake the task of delivering the expert opinion ("commission expert opinion"). Experts are not subject to cross-examination. If a party disagrees with the expert, it may apply for the appointment of a different expert.

A complex expert appraisal will be directed by the court if the establishment of the circumstances of the case requires the simultaneous performance of the studies with the involvement of various fields of knowledge or with the use of various lines of science in the framework of a single field of knowledge. A complex appraisal will be entrusted to several experts. Proceeding from the results of the studies carried out, the experts will formulate a joint opinion on the circumstances and render it in a report which will be signed by all the experts. A commission expert opinion will be appointed by the court for establishing the facts by two or more experts in a single field of knowledge. The experts will confer among themselves and, having reached a common opinion, formulate it and sign the report. An expert who disagrees with the other expert or other experts will have the right to present a separate report on all issues, or on the individual issue, which have caused the difference of opinion.

76. An expert is obliged to accept the assignment entrusted to him by the court, and to carry out an exhaustive study of all the submitted materials and documents; to present a substantiated and objective report on the questions put to him and to direct it to the court that has appointed the expert; to appear in court when summoned to personally take part in the court session and to answer questions connected with carrying out the expert appraisal and with the report he has submitted. The expert has no right to collect materials for conducting an expert appraisal on his own; to enter into personal contact with the parties to the proceedings if this puts into doubt his lack of interest in the outcome of the case; to divulge information which has become known to him in connection with carrying out the expert appraisal, or to inform anyone about the results of the appraisal, with the exception of the court that has directed it. An expert may not refuse to make an expert examination, commissioned thereto, within the period established by the court, by reason of a refusal of the party to pay for the expert examination before it has been conducted. The expert will have the right, insofar as it is necessary for him to submit the report, to become acquainted with the materials of the case concerning the object of the expert appraisal; to ask the court to supply him with additional materials and documents for the study; to put, in the court session, questions to the persons taking part in the case, and to the witnesses; and to file petitions inviting other experts to participate in conducting an expert appraisal. The expert will submit his report in writing. The expert's report will contain a detailed description of the study carried out, the conclusions he has arrived at as a result of it and the answers to the questions raised by the court. Complete acceptance of everything contained in the expert's report is not obligatory for the court and it will be evaluated along with other evidence.

If the court needs clarifications on any peculiar professional areas, it may also bring to the trial the specialists who have knowledge in special areas and who may provide the court with their advice and professional opinion. The specialists do not give their opinion in writing, instead they give their opinion only verbally.

Part VI. Particular Proceedings

Chapter 1. Administrative Procedure

77. In 2015, a new Code of Administrative Procedure was adopted in Russia. Such a code has never existed before in Russian legal history. Historically in Russia, in contrast to some other countries, as soon as cases stemming from administrative relations became an allowed subject for judicial inquiry, their hearing was included in civil procedure, and certain sections were added to the Code of civil procedure.[19]

In 1993, the Constitution of the Russian Federation established separate legal proceedings for civil, administrative and criminal cases. Administrative procedure did not exist in practice until 2015 although related amendments were already being proposed in the mid-1990s. The Code of Administrative Procedure was approved by the Russian President on March 9, 2015 and entered into force on September 15, 2015.

With the adoption of the new Code, a number of laws and regulations concerning legal proceedings for the investigation of administrative cases have changed. The provisions regulating proceedings arising out of administrative cases have been excluded from the Civil Procedural Code, along with provisions on consideration of applications for compensation due to violations of the right to legal proceedings within a reasonable time, and on compulsory hospitalization of citizens in psychiatric hospitals.

Unlike the codes of civil and commercial procedures, the Code of Administrative Procedure emphasizes the active role of the courts. This is motivated by the unequal positions of the parties in relevant cases. In particular, if necessary, the court can call for evidence itself, and it can go beyond the bases and arguments of the declared requirements when checking the legality of legal statutory acts, decisions, actions and omissions.

Another innovation of the Code is the demand for confirmation that the participants in a trial have a higher legal education. The parties to administrative proceedings will also have additional expenses. However, all expenses, including attorneys' fees, any state duty and other expenses connected with the proceedings will be borne by the defeated party. Therefore, it is quite possible that it will be more expedient for many potential plaintiffs to pay penalties rather than risk incurring additional expenses and spending time on an administrative trial. On the other hand, officials will sometimes have to think twice before making a decision, as those additional expenses can also be collected from the state, which could be very unpleasant for the government.

19. Dmitry Tumanov, *Public Interest and Administrative Legal Proceedings*, 3(3) Brics L.J. 64 (2016).

Finally, the new Code provides additional guarantees for access to justice, and it makes the procedure more professional and specialized.

Chapter 2. Class Actions

78. Among different types of group actions only public and organizational group actions are possible in Russia.

Since Soviet times, public group litigation has existed in Russia. The 2003 Civil Procedural Code provides for special regulation. According to its Article 45 the attorney general can go to court to defend the interests of an indefinite group of persons. Organizational group actions are regulated in the same manner by Article 46. These rules are expanded by special regulation in specific fields of law. For example, the Consumer Protection Law of 1992 (Article 46) and the Securities Law of 1999 (Article 19) contain similar rules to protect consumers rights. The problem is that the laws simply stipulate the right for the attorney general or organizations to sue. Specific (procedural) rules are not provided.

At the same time, there is a vibrant academic discussion[20] regarding the introduction of private group actions. This discussion started along with the beginning of judicial reform in the 1990s. The relevance of improvement of groups' rights protection mechanisms and mechanisms of protection of an unspecified number of persons are not called into question by the majority of procedure scholars. However, many researchers warn against the introduction of the Anglo-Saxon model of private class actions in Russia.

There have been several steps in the attempt to introduce private group actions in Russia. First, one option was offered while developing the Civil Procedural Code of 2003, but it was rejected by the working group.

79. Second, in July 2009 Federal Law No. 205-FZ "On amendments to certain acts of the Russian Federation" was adopted according to which the special order of case hearing on group rights and legitimate interests protection was established in the Arbitrazh (Commercial) Procedural Code. This law introduced quasi-private group actions. Special provisions (Chapter 28.2 "Consideration of the cases of protection of rights and legal interests of a group of persons") regulate the proceedings in such cases.

The claim has to concern not only personal but also collective rights of other participants and, additionally, it has to be supported by at least five persons. Only at observance of these two conditions will the case be heard according to these special rules of the Arbitrazh (Commercial) Procedural Code.

The person who appealed to the commercial court is the key participant in the class action proceedings. This person has the rights and performs the procedural duties of the claimant and is obliged to conscientiously protect the rights and legitimate interests of all members of the group. He can act without power of attorney, under documents on other persons' accession to the claim, which can be the written statement of one person or the decision of several persons to accession. His powers can be stopped due to his renunciation of suit, or on request of most of the members of the group. In case of discontinuance the court postpones the judicial proceedings for its replacement. He has to notify other members of group if the need arises for carrying out replacement independently. If no member of the group agrees to act as this person, the court stops the proceedings on the class action.

20. Dmitry Magonya, *Class Actions in Russia*, 1(1) Russian L.J. (2013).

80. Special rules of preparation for the court proceedings work for such cases as category hearings. The main specifics concern the procedure in respect of other persons joining in the statement of claim. In this stage the court has to define an order of formation of a group, joined to the claim. For this purpose it establishes the term during which it is necessary to make the proposal to other persons to join the class action and also the term during which these persons can join it.

The duty to make such proposal, and also to inform the court on the joined persons and to provide the relevant documents falls on the person who initially appealed to the court. Such offer is to be made publicly. The court determines the concrete way of placement of the offer but, by the general rule, it is published in the mass media, or goes by mail with recorded delivery. The expediency of such order raises doubts. First, the duty of notice is assigned not to the court, as is established for notice of participants in the case, but to the initiator of the claim. Second, the list of ways of notice is open, which allows to reduce them to a formality and by that to limit membership of the group.

The existing rules insufficiently clearly define the status of the persons joined to the claim. If the initiator of the claim has the rights of the claimant and performs the claimant's duties as it is directly specified in Article 225[12] of the Arbitrazh (Commercial) Procedural Code, the legal status of the joined persons is not defined.

81. The class action has to be considered within five months from the date of rendering of the ruling on the initiation of proceedings of a claim. The established procedure of filing and hearing of the class action raises a number of remarks. The general condition of filing of the claim gives the chance for various interpretations: members of the group, except for the initiator of the claim, have almost no procedural rights; it is unclear whether members of the group have the right to appeal the decision; etc.

Unlike the classic Anglo-Saxon model of private class actions where the participants in the group do not always have to be clearly defined during the hearing, the Russian Arbitrazh (Commercial) Procedural Code establishes a necessary condition—formation of a group prior to judicial proceedings, at a preparation stage. Such regulation changes the nature of the classic construction of the class action.

Therefore, on the one hand, the established procedure gives a chance to create a group, but, on the other hand—participants of this group have to be listed prior to the case hearing. Differences between this order and the institute of joinder of parties are minimum. The established rules of formation of a group do not contradict the norms of joinder of parties. Therefore, this procedure, in fact, is not an innovation of the Arbitrazh (Commercial) Procedural Code, it only concretizes the regulation of joinder of parties.

The third attempt to introduce private group actions in Russia is the initiative of the Federal Anti-competition Agency. Its group action amendments to the procedural codes and anti-competition legislation were drafted in 2012–2014.[21] According to its 2012 Road Map "Developing Competition and Improving Anti-competition Policy," group actions should be introduced before the courts of general jurisdiction as well as the commercial courts. Finally, the amendments were formulated in the draft of the federal law "On amendments to certain acts of the Russian Federation regarding

21. Dmitry Magonya, *Class Actions in Russia*, 1(1) Russian L.J. 63 (2013).

settlement of an order of case hearing on group rights and legitimate interests protection (group proceedings)," but this law was never adopted.

The fourth attempt, in 2015, was the adoption of a new Code of Administrative Procedure. Such a code has never existed before in Russia. The Code entered into force on September 15, 2015. As already mentioned, due to the adoption of the new Code, a number of laws and regulations concerning legal proceedings for the investigation of administrative cases have changed. One such novelty is the new regulation on group litigation under Article 42 "Collective administrative claim." According to this article, the court should initiate group proceedings if at least twenty persons have joined the claim. They must select a person who will participate in the proceedings on behalf of the group. If somebody has filed a similar claim with similar subject matter and grounds, the court proposes to join the collective claim. This procedure cannot truly be defined as group litigation, because it requires an exact number of parties. Rather, it should be considered more a joinder of parties.

Therefore, today Russian legislation consists of only organizational and public class actions. There were a few attempts to introduce private class actions, but they failed.

Part VII. Enforcement of Judgments

Chapter 1. Enforcement of Domestic Judgments

82. Winning a court case is usually not enough to obtain money or other relief from a debtor. It is only the beginning of a lengthy and challenging process of enforcement of court judgments and collecting debts. Therefore, the final part of a civil action is execution of the judgment. Without execution the goal of procedure is not achieved. The execution is regulated not only by the procedural codes, but also by special laws "On execution" (2007) and "On bailiffs" (1997).

83. There are four stages of the execution of the judgment: initiation of the execution, preparation for the implementation of measures of compulsory execution, implementation of measures of compulsory execution, and termination. The law provides for a general two-month deadline for the entire enforcement procedure. However, there are no sanctions for violation of this deadline, thus enforcement, in practice, could last much longer.

The initiation stage consists of the issuance of a writ of execution, its filing with the bailiff service and delivery of the court ruling on the initiation of the execution. The enforcement is mainly initiated on the basis of an enforcement order, which is issued by a court as soon as the decision comes into force. A writ of execution is the basic document which confirms the judgment creditor's right to enforce the court judgment. A writ of execution can be presented within three years from the entry of a judgment into legal force; however, the court has the power to grant an additional three months for presentation of the writ of execution. Writs of execution that contain requirements for periodic payments can be presented within the entire term for which payments are awarded, as well as within three years after the end of this term. A writ of execution is presented for enforcement at the place of execution of the judgment, which is usually the debtor's place of residence or the place where the debtor's property is located.

The preparation stage includes performance of the actions aiming at voluntary execution and establishment of the debtor and his property location. A five-day term for voluntary execution is established by a bailiff. After expiration of this period, enforcement is started. The debtor bears an enforcement fee (7% of the amount claimed) in a case of refusal of voluntary execution without reasonable cause. There also could be expenses for enforcement actions and bailiff's fines. The bailiff also send inquiries to different state and non-state authorities and agencies such as the tax service, the police and registration offices for searching the debtor's assets.

Implementation of the measures of compulsory execution consists of garnishment (seizure), property disposal and distribution of the collected money. The garnishment (seizure) includes performance of two obligatory actions such as taking inventory of assets and imposing an injunction on the rights of disposal thereof, and, if required, three optional actions such as restricting the right to use the property, the inventory of the property and a ban on disposal of the property. The amount obtained by the bailiff from the debtor is transferred for satisfying the creditors' claims in the following priority: first, claims regarding alimony and compensation for accidental and death-causing injuries; second, employees' claims arising out of contractual relations; third, claims regarding payments to state non-budget funds; and fourth, all other claims.

The termination can either be a return of the writ of execution without execution, or the termination of execution. The latter requires an additional court ruling.

84. There are a number of particular measures in Russian enforcement procedure. First, one of the most popular indirect enforcement measures of recent times is the prohibition to leave the country. This measure has been effective since 2007. The bailiff can prohibit the debtor from traveling abroad if the debt is more than RUR 10,000. This measure was performed in relation to 2 million debtors in 2016, 50% of them were claims regarding alimony.

It is necessary to note that unlike many countries criminal arrest of debtors in relation to civil cases is not used in Russia. This appeared in Russian case law in 2013.

Among indirect enforcement measures there is also *astreinte* (i.e., noncompliance penalty) in Russian legislation.[22]

A special enforcement procedure is established in relation to official state authorities if they act as debtors. This concerns the government, ministries, official agencies, etc. The general rules are excluded in this case, and special legal regulation has been established. The Budget Code (1998) provides the rules concerning the enforcement of such judgments. The Federal Bailiff Service does not have authority to enforce them. A writ of execution should be delivered to the Treasury Department, which acts as the enforcement organ.

Finally, there is some statistics (2015). There are 25,000 bailiffs in Russia. On average, about 2,200 cases are pending with each bailiff every year. Thirty million cases are initiated every year by the bailiffs. There were around 324,000 garnishments (seizures) of property performed by the bailiffs. In 2011 the Federal Bailiff Service created the Databank of enforcement cases. It contains information of all enforcement documents and is available online for the public.

22. Francesca Ferrari & Natalya Bocharova, *The Astreinte in the Italian and Russian Administrative (Judicial) and Civil Proceedings*, 3(3) Russian L.J. 24 (2015).

Chapter 2. Recognition and Enforcement of Foreign Judgments

85. Foreign judgments are recognized and enforced in Russia by courts of general jurisdiction as well as by arbitrazh courts. The procedure in both courts is not the same, but similar. In most cases the recognition of foreign judgments is the arbitrazh courts' competence, because they have jurisdiction over commercial disputes. Courts of general jurisdiction rarely consider such cases.

A procedure for recognition could be initiated if a multilateral international agreement exists or if a bilateral international agreement is concluded between Russia and the country where the judgment was rendered. Russia has numerous agreements including among others China, Greece, Spain, Belarus. Russia is also a party to the New York Convention of 1958.[23]

The enforcement of a foreign judgment is possible during three years after it was rendered. Venue is usually determined by reference to the residence of the defendant. Article 412 of the Civil Procedural Code states the grounds for refusal of recognition: (1) the judgment has not yet entered into legal force; (2) the parties have not been notified about the case; (3) there is a judgment or a dispute between the same parties and the same subject matter; (4) the recognition and enforcement of the foreign judgment could violate the public policy of Russia. Violation of public policy means the difference between the legislation of Russia and a foreign country that can threaten the rights of citizens or legal entities in Russia.

23. Convention of 1958 on the Recognition and Enforcement of Foreign Arbitral Awards.

Part VIII. Arbitration

Chapter 1. Legislation

86. First of all, it should be kept in mind that justice in the Russian Federation is conducted solely by courts, which means that no other authority other than the court has the power to render an obligatory decision to parties at trial.

Russia is a party to the New York Convention on the Recognition and Enforcement of Foreign Arbitral Awards. The USSR was one of the original Member States to sign the convention in 1958. There is a distinction between international and domestic arbitration. Arbitration in Russia is regulated by Federal Law "On Arbitral Tribunals in the Russian Federation" (2003) (domestic arbitration), and also by Federal Law "On International Commercial Arbitration" (1993) (international arbitration); this law was drafted on the basis of the UNCITRAL Model Law on International Commercial Arbitration.

87. Most arbitration in Russia is institutional. Ad hoc procedures are not popular. There are around 500 arbitral institutions in Russia and only seven to ten of them could be considered important, with their own set of rules and the option of cross-border disputes resolution. Such leading institution is the International Commercial Arbitration Court (ICAC) at the Chamber of Commerce and Industry of the Russian Federation in Moscow. Its history dates back to 1932 when the USSR founded the Foreign Trade Arbitration Commission. It is the most frequently used court for international arbitration in Russia and handles an average of 200–250 cases per year. In 2013, the National Russian Arbitration Association was created as an independent arbitration institution and an alternative to ICAC.

The previous system of arbitration had several disadvantages. One of them was the dramatic increase in the number of arbitral institutions over the last fifteen years. Many arbitral institutions were established by major corporations and are influenced by them; this is known as a "pocket" arbitration.

The most recent reform of arbitration in Russia started in 2014. The first draft law on arbitration was introduced by the Russian Ministry of Justice in January 2014, but it was returned by the government for revision. In May 2015, the government introduced a revised draft law in parliament. Finally, the President signed Federal Law "On Arbitration in the Russian Federation" and Federal Law "On Changes to Related Laws of the Russian Federation." The first law regulates domestic arbitration, while the second concerns international arbitration.

There are three important aspects of the recent reform: first, the arbitrability of corporate disputes; second, the more detailed regulation of the arbitral proceedings; and third, the licensing of the arbitral institutions.

Corporate disputes were non-arbitrable before the reform. This rule was stipulated not by the legislation but by court practice. The new laws determine the arbitrability of this category of disputes. However, there are some limitations. For example, the seat of arbitration of corporate disputes must be only in Russia.

The new laws establish a number of administrative requirements for arbitral institutions. They introduce very strict rules of arbitration. The new laws are similar to procedural codes. State courts have more influence over arbitration, which could eventually lose its effectiveness as an alternative form of state litigation. Many details are now stipulated in the legislation. For example, the duty of an arbitral institution is to publish information about its cases on the internet.

Most of the institutions must obtain the licenses provided by the government. All foreign arbitral institutions should also obtain certification from the government. The new Council of Arbitral Development is established under the supervision of the Ministry of Justice. It gives preliminary approval in the licensing proceedings. In general, the new laws make ad hoc arbitration less preferable than institutional arbitration due to the increasing control by the state courts over them as well as a number of restrictive rules; for example, by excluding ad hoc arbitration in corporate dispute resolution.

There are other novelties in the laws. They allow retired judges to act as arbitrators. There is also a very important regulation that clarifies that a foreign arbitral award, which does not require enforcement, is recognized in Russia automatically without any recognition proceedings.

It could be concluded that the general trend of the reform is the increasing state control over arbitration. However, the new regulation is very important; it makes huge changes and could be qualified as the start of a new era in arbitration in Russia.

Chapter 2. Arbitrability

88. The general rule of arbitrability states that any dispute is arbitrable unless otherwise directly stated by law. The following disputes cannot be resolved by arbitration, but only by state commercial courts: corporate disputes (before 2016; *see supra* Part IX Chapter 1.); intellectual property disputes; bankruptcy; public law disputes, among others. There is also a risk of non-arbitrability of other types of disputes due to the lack of legal regulation and different courts' interpretations. For example, Russian courts recently confirmed that disputes arising from government-related contracts are not arbitrable.

Chapter 3. Arbitral Tribunal

89. The arbitrators cannot be state court judges; if the panel consists of three members, then at least one of them should be a lawyer. It is possible to appoint foreign nationals as arbitrators in international arbitral proceedings. A court cannot intervene in the selection of arbitrators. An arbitral tribunal can decide on its own jurisdiction.

Chapter 4. Conduct of Arbitral Proceedings

90. The parties have the right to agree on the procedure to be followed by the arbitral tribunal in conducting proceedings. Parties are free to agree on a language other than Russian being used in the proceedings.

Chapter 5. Arbitral Award and Enforcement

91. An arbitration award cannot be appealed. A party can make an application to the competent court for enforcement of the award and that application should be heard within three months.

Part IX. Mediation

Chapter 1. Legislation

92. The first Russian legislation on mediation was introduced in 2011. Federal Law "Alternative Procedures for Dispute Settlement with participation of a mediator (mediation procedure)" (2011) establishes the procedures for mediation.

Chapter 2. Rights That Can Be Subject to Mediation

93. Mediation procedure can be applied after the occurrence of disputes transferred for consideration in civil proceedings and proceedings in arbitrazh (commercial) courts. Mediation procedure is applied neither to collective labor disputes nor to disputes that can affect the rights of third parties not participating in the mediation procedure, or public interests.

Mediation may be undertaken according to the mutual will of the parties, on the basis of the principles of voluntariness, confidentiality, cooperation and equal rights of the parties, and the impartiality and independence of the mediator.

Chapter 3. Mediation Agreement

94. A mediation agreement is a written agreement between the parties concluded prior to the occurrence of a dispute or when a dispute has arisen to have recourse to mediation in order to resolve the dispute which has arisen or can arise between the parties in relation to some specific legal relationship. A mediation agreement will contain data: (1) about the subject of the dispute; (2) about the mediator; and (3) about conditions for the parties' payment of costs connected with the provision of mediation procedure.

Chapter 4. Mediator

95. A mediator is an independent individual engaged by the parties as intermediary in dispute resolution with the objective of assisting them to reach a decision themselves, as the parties, on the merits of the dispute.

Chapter 5. Mediation Procedure

96. If the parties have entered into an agreement to use mediation procedure, during the period stipulated for the mediation procedure the parties are obliged not to apply to the court for the resolution of the dispute that has occurred. The court will acknowledge this obligation until the conditions of the said obligation are executed, save for the case where either of the parties, in the party's opinion, has to protect its rights. If a dispute is referred to the court, the parties may apply mediation procedure at any moment before a decision on the dispute is made by the relevant court.

During the process of mediation all information relating to the mediation will be considered confidential, save in cases provided by federal laws and in cases where the parties have agreed otherwise. The mediator has no right to disclose information concerning mediation procedure or the information that became known to him during mediation without the consent of the parties.

Chapter 6. Settlement Agreement

97. A settlement agreement is an agreement reached by the parties as the result of application of mediation procedure in relation to a dispute or disputes or different disagreements concerning a dispute. A settlement agreement is concluded in written form and should contain data on the parties, the subject matter of the dispute, the mediation procedure performed, the name of the mediator, as well as the obligations agreed, and the terms and conditions of their performance. It will be executed on the basis of the principles of voluntariness and the good faith of the parties. If it is arrived at by the parties as the result of mediation procedure, carried out after transfer of the dispute to a court or for arbitration consideration, it can be confirmed by the court or arbitration as an amicable settlement agreement according to the procedural legislation.

Conclusion

98. The global era of today is the time of the increased role of civil justice. Different procedural systems are spread across the modern world. The most common are the Continental, Anglo-Saxon and mixed systems. The frontier between the two classic models of civil procedure has blurred, and it appears that a unified procedural system is emerging. At the same time, some distinctive and unique procedural systems still exist. The Russian system of civil procedure is one of them.

Selected Bibliography

Berman, Harold. *Justice in the USSR: An Interpretation of Soviet Law*. (1963).

Butler, William. *Russian Law*. (2009).

Cappelletti, Mauro. "Social and Political Aspects of Civil Procedure: Reforms and Trends in Western and Eastern Europe". *Mich. L. Rev.*, vol. 69 (1971).

Chenworth, Don W. "Soviet Civil Procedure: History and Analysis". *Trans. Amer. Phil. Soc.*, vol. 67 (1977).

Conlon, Brian. "Dostoevsky v. the Judicial Reforms of 1864 : How and Why One of Nineteenth-Century Russia 's Greatest Writers Criticized the Nation's Most Successful Reform". *Russian L.J.*, vol. 2, no. 4 (2014).

Ferrari, Francesca & Natalya Bocharova. "The Astreinte in the Italian and Russian Administrative (Judicial) and Civil Proceedings" *Russian L.J.*, vol. 3, no. 3 (2015).

Maleshin, Dmitry. "The Russian Style of Civil Procedure". *Emory Intl. L. Rev.*, vol. 21 (2007).

Osakwe, Christopher. "The Public Interest and the Role of the Procurator in Soviet Civil Litigation: A Critical Analysis". *Tex. Intl. L.J.*, vol. 18 (1983).

Quigley, John. "Socialist Law and the Civil Law Tradition". *Am. J. Comp. L.*, vol. 37, no. 4 (1989).

Reshetnikova, Irina. "Judicial Reforms in Russia: 1864 to 2014". *Russian L.J.*, vol. 3, no. 2 (2015).

Solomon, Peter. "Judicial Power in Russia: Through the Prism of Administrative Justice". *L. & Socy. Rev.*, vol. 38, no. 3 (September 2004).

Tumanov, Dmitry. "Public Interest and Administrative Legal Proceedings". *Brics L.J.*, vol. 3, no. 3 (2016).

van der Pol, Ruth & Anton Petrov. "Searching for Truth in Civil Process: The Netherlands and Russia". *Russian L.J.*, vol. 3, no. 1 (2015).

Vyshinsky, Andrei. *The Law of the Soviet State*. (1948).

Selected Bibliography

Index

The numbers here refer to paragraph numbers.

Index

Made in the USA
Monee, IL
13 September 2026

62974276R00050